SHE IS SITTING IN THE NIGHT

Re-visioning Thea's Tarot

SHE IS SITTING IN THE NIGHT

Re-visioning Thea's Tarot

Oliver Pickle

Art by Ruth West
Foreword by Rima Athar

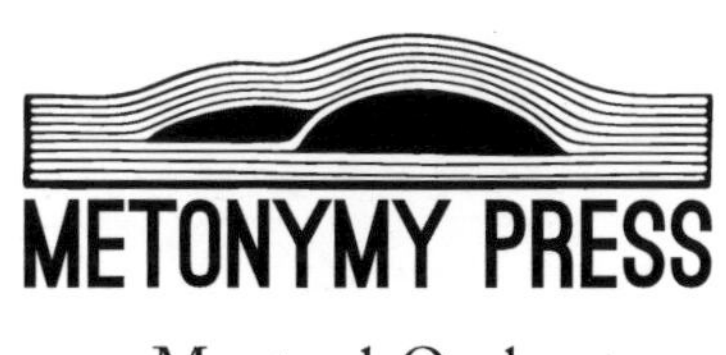

Montreal, Quebec

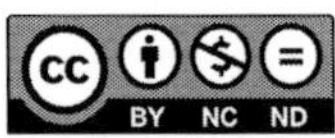

First edition
Printed and bound in Canada by Imprimerie Gauvin
Cover design by Nazik Dakkach (using original image by Ruth West)
Editing and interior book design by Ashley Fortier
Sixth Printing - 2020 (First Printing - 2015)

Published by Metonymy Press
PO Box 143 BP Saint Dominique
Montreal, QC H2S 3K6
Canada
metonymypress.com

Library and Archives Canada Cataloguing in Publication

Pickle, Oliver, 1983-, author
She is sitting in the night : re-visioning Thea's Tarot / Oliver Pickle; art by Ruth West ; foreword by Rima Athar.

ISBN 978-0-9940471-0-6 (paperback)

1. Major arcana (Tarot). 2. Minor arcana (Tarot). 3. Tarot cards. 4. Lesbians. 5. Feminism. I. Title.

BF1879.T2P52 2015 133.3'2424086643 C2015-903019-6

To the person who brought me my first deck and then regretted it. To Josh and Bill, who really nurtured the art in Winnipeg that summer—the former by leaving me in his house filled with plants and animal remains, and the latter by suggesting Pollack's text. To Zoë and Jay, for cider and tarot nights ad infinitum.

To Steph, Tanya, Kay, Mel, and Jessika, who read the manuscript. To Devon, for starting to edit the book with me on the deck of the cabin, and for seeing the possibilities in everything. To Ruth, for the deck. To Rima, for the impetus. To Ashley, who finally asked me for a reading last summer.

Contents

MAJOR ARCANA

MINOR ARCANA

FOREWORD

Rima Athar

Searching for a Lesbian Feminist Tarot Deck

The story of this book really begins when I did an online search for a lesbian feminist tarot deck. I'd been increasingly interested in the tarot as a guide for working through day-to-day emotional struggles. I saw the practice as being situated within a larger tradition of knowledge sharing that centres the human spirit, of energies and intuition, and of an understanding of our place as intimately connected to nature, both on earth and within the cosmos. For example, the I Ching (Book of Changes), one of the more ancient Chinese divination texts, uses divination by numbers in a similar manner. Combinations of numbers and their place in our mathematical understanding of the universe are related to both cosmological patterns of energy flows as well as human value systems, such as the concepts of balance and Yin Yang. The I Ching has also been visually represented as a 64-card deck, used similarly to the tarot.

Yet while I see tarot as a tool for exploring the universal human experience, the mainstream decks I came across were overwhelmingly laden with symbolism and iconography associated with hierarchical European monarchies, with themes of conquest and war, dogmatic Christian religious orthodoxy, and moral overtones. While Strength and the High Priestess in the Major Arcana are often depicted as independent female figures, I was struck by how few women were represented overall in the 78 cards. The Empress is followed by the Emperor, and the four Queens of the Minor Arcana are ultimately subservient to the Kings. In many of the interpretations I came across, the Queens seemed to symbolize either cold and calculating or overly emotional forces to be wary of. The more I looked at the artwork within various decks, the more the representations seemed to reflect a conspicuously absent story. Like so much of history that is rewritten by erasing what came before, I was sure there had to be decks that reflected a different worldview, a feminist worldview.

When I came across archived images of Thea's Tarot by Ruth West, I knew I had found just that. Here was a deck full of hella-queer women: lesbians in flannel shirts, holding hands, having picnics, writing ideas down, sharing food, gardening, and making all sorts of love. Here were women of many shapes and sizes and colours, from historical and contemporary walks of life, basking in the glory of day-to-day life.

Interspersed with the everyday scenes were representations of more fantastical, mythical, and spiritual beings. These were usually figured within the Major Arcana, along with some of the more emotionally charged cards within the Minor Arcana (for a more detailed explanation of themes within the Major and Minor Arcana, see the interpretative notes, pp. 21–27). The Tower and the Comet, for example, show figures being swept up in the currents and tides that govern planets and stars, elements that pay homage to astrology as a reminder of our minor place within the universe, and the impossibility of being fully in control.

What held the deck together was the recurrence of certain symbols and iconography: the mountains, trees, and plants; living rooms, kittens, and bedrooms; aviator sunglasses, jewellery, and patterned clothing; the arch of an eyebrow, the sideways glances, the expressiveness in the hands and fingers and faces. Symbols to which we can all relate. And all of this was conveyed through the intricacy of papercut design, in which each element within the image connects to another. Think stencils, but on a smaller scale, where what is cut out is actually what gives shape, emphasis, and weight to the image as a whole.

Designing a Queer Tarot Book

Self-published by Ruth West in 1984, Thea's Tarot seemed like a true gem. I tried to order it, only to realize it was out of print. It took a few more months, but I kept searching for a copy of the deck. Eventually I happened upon an online forum—already three years out of date—where someone had found Ruth West. I emailed her in the hopes that the address was still valid. It was, and Ruth still had some copies of the deck. I remember how good it felt when the cards were in my hands a few weeks later. When I finally had the chance to interview Ruth, I learned I wasn't the only one who'd been on something of a journey to find her deck. She related to me,

> Honestly, it's a bit of a cult deck. I launched it at a time when there were a lot of woman-centred decks coming out—there were three in that year alone. So on its launch it didn't actually get as much attention as I would have hoped. But in the years that followed, I started noticing that people from all over would somehow make their way to the deck. It definitely seems to speak to a niche audience, who are looking for something different. And even now, when it's been out of print for two decades or more, I still get two to three people a year emailing me to ask for copies.

When I received the deck, it came with an A4-sized pamphlet that had little in the way of explanation, apart from a few words about each card. The simplicity spoke to me of possibility, of a politics of letting the reader interpret the cards and imagery as they wished, without putting stringent limits on the audience's reading.

It was the intersection of the politics that leaped off the cards, the creative space made by a lack of a detailed guide, and the fact that the deck was out of print that spurred my desire to create a book. I wanted it to be at once an archival documentation of lesbian feminist art history from the 1980s, as well as a revival of the spirit of reclaiming and re-defining ways of meaning making. I wanted to reproduce the artwork, and through it to explore stories of what a queer feminist tarot could look like in terms of today's sexual and gender politics.

Of course, revisiting lesbian feminist histories from the 1970s and 1980s, and reinterpreting artwork from that era to reflect a more current queer feminist politics in the 2010s, is not without its challenges. How exactly do you make a lesbian deck queer? How do you play with gender in a way that still respects the woman-centred focus of the deck, while allowing room for a politics of fluid gender boundaries? How do you address and represent images and/or perspectives that may come across as challenging, especially if you don't know enough of the history? Perhaps most importantly, how do you do all that, while keeping it fun, playful, and down to earth?

Thea's Tarot: History, Art, Design, Politics

Those were the conversations we were having when I asked Oliver—tarot reader to many queers in Montreal—if they would write the book for me. While Oliver started ruminating on the shape it would take, I sought out Ruth West again. It took another year to track her down the second time, but when I pitched the project, she graciously and charmingly accepted. From there we had a series of Skype conversations, during which Ruth discussed with me the deck's history, her artistic process, and even tidbits about romance, astrology, stages of growth and love, and the sexual and gender politics that come out so clearly in some of cards:

> The starting point for Thea's Tarot was actually another guidebook, *A New Women's Tarot*, which was a hand-stapled, self-published pamphlet put out by Billie Potts and Elf and Dragons Press in 1977. Billie Potts was really my mentor in creating this deck, and in her *New Women's Tarot*, she went through each card and rebranded it with feminist matriarchal iconography. It was a very specific way of talking about these ideas of women's spiritual and historical power. What I really liked about her book was that it gave descriptions of the tarot without pictures, so that looking at it you could then build your own concepts from what was written.
>
> The deck took four years to make. I didn't do it consecutively. I would come to it now and again, flip through *A New Women's Tarot* and come across a card description at random. Whatever one jumped out at me that day, I would sit with the ideas, ruminate on it, and figure how it spoke to me. Like saying, "Okay, this is what I'm feeling and

> where I am today," and from there I would begin composing the imagery, the layout, the iconography.
>
> In fact, the whole deck was two-tone colour originally. And I self-published it, pre-computer, pre-scanner! I was looking for a new project, and I came across papercut as a medium I was drawn to artistically, as something to sit and do, and to meditate and create with. Every card was cut in two tone, then each one shot with a camera, printed and then reduced into black and white copy, and then laid out. It was a real labour of love, from 1980 to 1984.

When Ruth graduated from college, she was in the midst of the 1970s feminist arts movement, which in exploring the intersections of arts and freedom of expression was reclaiming a space for women's experiences. There was a surge in a do-it-yourself ethos; the opening of women-run arts centres, publishing houses, festivals, and conferences; and a movement for collective organizing.

> It was a personal process. I was fresh from college, in my mid-20s, and I had recently come out as a lesbian. Lesbian feminism was a big deal at the time. I was searching around for meaning, and looking at the world in which I'd been directed one way my whole life, and challenging those ideas. It was a period of self-discovery.
>
> Right after college, I had helped work to install Judy Chicago's *The Dinner Party* when it toured in Boston. I was completely immersed in women's art, discussing women's art. There were so many of us, looking at ourselves as artists and saying "Why aren't we out there?" And then in the midst of the glass ceiling, you had the Guerrilla Girls coming out in 1986 to denounce the MOMA.
>
> So that was the ethos of that time period. There was lots of crafts culture, making art, jewellery, clothes. Going to festivals, sharing food. We were really coming into our own rights and politics. We were finding strength in who we were as women, and redefining our identities as people.

A Tribute to Goddess Cultures

When we talked of representational practices, the theme that stood out was the importance given to reclaiming body politics and matriarchal cultures, as well as the tribute to goddesses, as the influences behind the imagery. There are a diversity of women represented in the deck. For example, the Three of Wands reflects Native American iconography; the Emperor is depicted as an Egyptian Pharaoh; and there is the central archetype of the Amazons, the historical/mythical nation of female warriors.

> It was really important to me to give life to women's bodies in all shapes and sizes. There purposely isn't just one body type in there, it's not a deck of thin women. And there are women from different backgrounds. My own background is Anglo-Saxon. I don't believe you should just take on other people's cultures, and it's important to pay attention to that within art and representation. Making this deck at age 26, my influences sit within what was happening at that moment, in the US. I was born in 1956, at the height of the post-war, baby-boomer generation. We were just after the hippies, but there was a really strong feminist youth culture happening. And more and more of us were figuring out how to define where we wanted our lives to be, what other options were out there. We were learning about women's histories and experiences all over.
>
> I really drew strongly from Billie Potts' historical referencing of different matriarchal and woman-centred archetypes in *A New Women's Tarot*. That book changed the cards to Mother, Daughter, Amazon, and Child. The archetype of the Amazon is that of the female warriors, of women as the protectors. It was a very current archetype in that era. The Emperor is also taken directly from *A New Women's Tarot*, which in relating women's roles as rulers in history highlighted Hatshepsut. She was one of the longest-ruling female Pharaohs of Ancient Egypt. The Three of Swords you mentioned, that's inspired by female Celtic Druids.
>
> So I got a lot from what was already in *A New Women's Tarot*, but also my own interests at the time. The central focus of my undergraduate work as an art major was actually

exploring the gods and goddesses of Greek and Roman mythology, along with Norse and English folklore. Thea is actually the Greek word for goddess. It was also the name of my cat, who you see in many of the cards.

Working through Challenges

Learning about the history of the deck was an engaging process, which raised a lot of questions, ideas, and conversations about feminisms, art, politics, and histories. I think for all of us—Ruth, Oliver, and myself—there have been parts of this process that made us step outside our comfort zones, and that challenged our perspectives. As Ruth shared with me,

> Thea's Tarot is a representation of a subset of time and space. It's like taking a photograph of my life and the politics around me at that moment. We did those things, thought those things, we looked at life that way.
>
> When you do something at a certain time period, it sets you there, and you forget that things move on, and your life grows and changes, and it may not look at all like it did when you were doing it. I was 26 when I launched the deck, and I'm 58 now. My life is in an entirely different place; I'm an entirely different person!
>
> Everything I am now builds on that, but it was a launching point. I think in revisiting this deck, with all of the questions about that era and those politics, you realize you cannot time-cast it through to the present day. It evolves.

There are details we might not all have agreed upon, but for me it was the process of having those intergenerational conversations, of taking each other's perspectives into account, and of building trust that made this project worth doing. What really brought this together was Oliver writing a book that gave space and voice to all of that, while also making us laugh.

The rest of this story lies in what's ahead: Oliver's introduction to their process in writing this book (pp. 17–19), more detailed information on the themes within tarot (pp. 21–27), and the guide to each of the cards (beginning on p. 31).

I want to give a big shout-out and thanks to the people who made this happen:

To Oliver, for bringing their unique perspectives to this project, for dedicating the time to writing this book and bringing it to life, and for having tough conversations when needed—there's no one else who could have translated the concept into as fun and playful a form;

To Ruth, for her support of the project, for generously agreeing to let us reproduce her beautiful artwork, and for taking the time to share her artistic process, her life experiences, her takes on sex, gender, politics, and more;

And of course to Ashley and Oliver as Metonymy Press, for their energy and investment in shaping this book collectively.

Introduction

I made a patchwork blanket the summer after my first painful breakup. *She Is Sitting in the Night* was pieced together in similar circumstances and was similarly possible during a mourning period. In the winter of January 2013 I was deeply sad and also devoted to writing daily, and my friend Rima had lent me her new tarot deck, Thea's Tarot. She asked if I would write descriptions of the cards for an eventual book project, as it had come with only a small pamphlet with one-line descriptions.[1] I got to work. Sometimes I couldn't make myself write for the time I'd allotted myself per day, but I could pull a single card and add to the slowly growing collection of descriptions that eventually became this book. (This process mirrored Ruth's original artistic process, discussed in Rima's foreword, though I wasn't aware of that at the time.)

It is a beautiful deck, and I added it to my repertoire, doing readings in Vancouver that spring on the patio of a pizza place on Main, in Montreal weekly at a tattoo and barber shop, and at the parks and kitchen tables where I regularly find myself, talking people through life. People responded to Thea's Tarot positively, and I found it in many ways to be less jarring and more appealing than the royalty-heavy, unavoidably gendered traditional decks. Here were homos lying naked on top of each other and holding hands, elders who were explicitly not kings, and images of fat, defiant queers.

There are a lot of alternatives to traditional decks, and there is a wealth of history of individuals and communities claiming and revising the tarot to suit their contexts; however, you have to remember that tarot decks are given, not sought out, and this is one of the many beautiful decks that were lent to me. Rima's excitement about it, the possibilities in

1 Excerpts from the Thea's Tarot pamphlet, written by Margaret Cleveland, are included below each card name in this book's card descriptions.

the black and white images, and the expression and variation in the bodies and faces and imagery on Ruth's feminist deck were impressive to me. The papercut style, the smell of the cards, the residue they left on each other, and the stark but comforting spreads they made all appealed to me.

Looking at the cards more closely and interpreting somebody else's 30-year-old artwork (which in itself was an interpretation of someone else's descriptions of the 78 cards) proved to be difficult at times. Though I eventually learned more about Ruth's artistic process, she didn't have answers for all of our questions about it, as—again—it took place decades ago. The way I read one person's depictions of global goddess imagery is unlikely to match their intentions, or the source imagery. I had questions about cultural representation and appropriation that no doubt would have been framed differently had they been asked at the time of the deck's production, or by someone besides myself.[2]

Rima and I, in conversation with Metonymy Press, decided that the value of the deck was substantial, and that recognizing some of our community's roots in the matriarchal, feminist, and queer inspirations and images of which Thea's Tarot is made up was an important if at times surprising and inconjunct process. As the current interpreter, I've called up what I find valuable in Ruth's representations, and interpreted according to my frameworks, which are queer, and gender-nonconforming, and antiauthoritarian, and attempting to undermine structural inequality. Sometimes this took the shape of using a variety of words to refer to breasts or chests, as people around me do in self-description. Sometimes it meant conversations about who was being sexualized in my descriptions and who was not. With input from Rima, it also meant assigning pronouns to the figures on the cards, which were definitively not always the ones that would have been chosen by the artist. But those are big tasks, and this is one deck, and I hope I have done it and those commitments justice. The deck's history and the centring of feminine-spectrum imagery and experiences are also reflected in the title choice.

---

2 The Amazon cards specifically stood out to some of our early readers. The reference to historical or mythical female warriors came from the reference book that was used to create Thea's Tarot, but it's a term so heavy with associations that many of us wouldn't choose it if we were creating a deck today.

This is fundamentally Rima's project, for me; I am the one who was familiar enough with tarot to interpret the deck further for her. I worked on these descriptions in the wake of casual tarot study over the past many years. I have been heavily influenced by *Seventy-Eight Degrees of Wisdom* and to a lesser extent by the Collective Tarot guidebook and the Winnipeg Tarot booklet, as well as a phone app and some websites, when I needed further explanation.

My own history with tarot started with The Mythic Tarot, brought back from San Francisco as a joke. I have mostly read in bars or on bedspreads, late at night, or holding down the cards on picnic tables or on the grass in parks, while my friends played baseball or gossiped. The first time I did readings for the public, it was in a small tent at a street festival during the anniversary celebration of La Centrale, an artist-run centre with whom Metonymy also collaborated this past year. Things really come full circle, and I can honour that while continuing to be a bit flippant with the practice of tarot in general.

My blithe attitude toward tarot is what has made me able to choose to do readings and to use the cards at all. I hope it has also in some way allowed me to introduce its possibilities for analysis and healing to people who would have otherwise shied away from it. The tone of the manuscript for this book received critique for this reason—however, if it weren't for the approach that underlies that tone, it wouldn't have been written at all.

I hope that the informed but casual queering of an already subversive revisionist deck will be inviting to those unfamiliar with the tarot. I also hope that it, without being comprehensive, honours and contributes something to those who take it seriously, which I clearly do deep down inside. Please enjoy.

- Oliver

INTERPRETATIVE NOTES

Tarot decks, including Thea's Tarot, contain Major and Minor Arcana cards, the latter of which mirror a standard playing-card four-suit configuration, probably due to their alleged historical purpose as playing cards.[1] There are 78 cards in the tarot (22 Major Arcana, including 0, and 56 Minor Arcana).

Major Arcana

The Major Arcana grab us and hit us where it hurts—in our archetypes. These cards mark the cycle of experience, from open possibility (Innocence), to controlled achievement (the Chariot), to taking pain and joy in equal measure and with equanimity (Grace), and healing and wholeness (the World). There are a few bumps along the way.

There are three parts of the Major Arcana in a psychology framework: the outer world, the inner life, and finally enlightenment. The cards of the Major Arcana may be thought of as individual archetypes, the central and guiding experiences we all share in cyclical ways, and they may also be laid out in a journey according to their numbering. In the first section, you face the external paraphernalia of life—exerting will onto the world, learning, creating relationships. In the second, you turn away from external striving and begin to self-reflect and address your inner life. In the third section of the Major Arcana, you become whole, able to exist consciously as a self while remaining connected in real and infinite ways to the universal. Cards 1–7 focus on outer life and striving, cards 8–14 on inner life and reflection, and cards 15–21 on the path to enlightenment, or something like that.

1 See, e.g., Rachel Pollack's *Seventy-Eight Degrees of Wisdom: A Book of Tarot* for a discussion of the potential origins of the deck as well as of its use for divination.

When Major Arcana are predominant in a divinatory reading, it's likely that you're going through some fundamentally life-changing times. If there are more Minor Arcana cards, your question and/or current experience is probably more momentary and related to your daily life.

Minor Arcana

In divinatory readings, the Minor Arcana (divided into the suits of wands, cups, swords, and pentacles) mark the daily, passing experiences of life, and are numbered Ace to ten, with four face cards.

Suits

Wands

The suit of wands is ruled by fire, and therefore by the impetus for—the essence of—life itself. Wands are an optimistic suit and symbolize passion, fighting to win, creative energy, and spirit. Fire, obviously, can also quickly destroy. Whether through overachievement or by ploughing down others in an enthusiastic frenzy, it can really be too much. Fire at its most effective aligns itself with the other elements, contributing struggle, action, and hope.

Cups

Love rules the water suit of the tarot, which is at the intersection of emotional and creative life. Water is an apt metaphor, in its changeability, for the way we emotionally blend with each other and adapt to the containers and environments in which we find ourselves. Water also symbolizes, in its constancy, how our inner lives may remain consistent, if mobile, below the surface of our actions and circumstances. Cups are receptive, and in these cards you'll find everything from receiving gifts to absorbing and moving through loss. Furthermore, you'll find reception to the point of passivity, and moving with and feeling things to a depressive point of inaction. Given the security it needs, the suit of cups is also where we experience interconnectedness—as water represents the unconscious and therefore the feeling that our experiences overlap beyond our individual connections—bringing us back to the love underlying and giving meaning to all major events and stages of life.

Swords

Swords are the suit of truth but also of sorrow, a combination with which I'm sure we're all familiar. With a weapon as a symbol for the air suit, pain or at least some conflict is bound to be wrapped up in it. Swords rule communication, intellect, rationality—the qualities associated with the mental suit of air—which, taken to extremes, without input or balance of the other suits' qualities (emotional depth or sensitivity, spirit or optimism, work or connection to nature), can be cutting, cruel, and downright destructive. Swords at their best allow us to assimilate and analyze our environment, communicate effectively, and take action based on clarity.

Pentacles

Earth is the element behind the pentacles suit. So here we have the container, the product, the goods, the $$$, the body, work, and of course the earth itself—basically the senses, the physical world, and overall, creation. While pentacles are often associated with money, from excessive greed to poverty to making steady wages, they are much more nuanced than that. Because earth is so tangible, it allows for real connection and creation, and finding magic and beauty in the mundane. This is where the action, feelings, and plans of the other suits are put into practice, where we work on projects, build physical and metaphoric foundations, and exist in a daily way. In pentacles we are greedy, shut-down workaholics at our worst, and generous, grounded artists and providers at our best.

Numbers

Ace : Opens us up to the raw energy of a suit and its element. The Ace holds the gifts or promises of each suit and asks you to grasp onto their energy, which is particularly strong when an Ace comes up in a reading.

Two : Represents unification ultimately leading to fulfilment; balance or imbalance.

Three : Often a complete expression of its suit, in a different way than are the tens (end of a cycle) or the Mothers (full external control).

Four : Always signifies structure and/or entrapment.

Five : Conflict, but also communication. All of the fives deal with loss.

Six : Communication and integration.

Seven : Victory, but also the imbalance of waiting and desire that precede it.

Eight : Grounded expression, tapping into cycles.

Nine : Fully cognizant and represents attainment, accumulation, experience, completion, compromise, and struggle.

Ten : Final expression of the suit (verging on near-boredom in repetition or closure). The end of a cycle, often unaware of its abundance.

Face Cards

Thea's Tarot uses the terms Child, Amazon, Daughter, and Mother instead of the more conventional (and sexist, royal) equivalents Page, Knight, Queen, and King. In a reading, Children, Amazons, Daughters, and Mothers either draw out their qualities in you or indicate someone in your life who takes on or represents the qualities of the card for you.

Child : A student- or child-like energy. Children are the messengers of their suits, starting and communicating the complexities of their whole expression.

Amazon : The Amazons in general are persevering, if not longsighted. As the teenagers of their suits, usually they don't express loyalty or other qualities with staying power. Restless and energetic, they plough through without much of a plan.

Daughter : Daughters represent a mature, balanced, wise internalization of each suit's qualities.

Mother : Mothers tend toward the most structured, external, social expression of each suit's qualities.

She Is Sitting in the Night and Thea's Tarot

This book can be used for tarot interpretation of any deck, and if you have it in combination with Thea's Tarot, you'll be able to match the images described. If the imagery veers quite far from the standard for a particular card, that difference is mentioned in the description.

In Thea's Tarot, card 8 is Justice and 11 is Strength. In many decks, these are in the opposite order, with Strength coming before Justice. Major Arcana card names specific to Thea's Tarot (with more conventional names for the same card in parentheses) are listed below:

0. Innocence (The Fool)
2. The Seer (The High Priestess)
3. The Creator (The Empress)
10. The Comet (Wheel of Fortune)
12. Art (The Hanged Man)
13. The Juggler (Death)
14. Grace (Temperance)
15. Oppression (The Devil)
20. Rebirth (Judgment)

Doing Tarot Readings

There are many reading formats and styles, and because I am a bit stodgy I've usually used the classic Celtic Cross formation. This ten-card reading brings the person asking the question (often called the querent) from where they are now, through the obvious and less obvious influences and motivations, and to their final outcome with a stop at their hopes and fears.

This is what it looks like. I usually lay the cards face down and then turn them one by one, connecting their meanings into a kind of story.

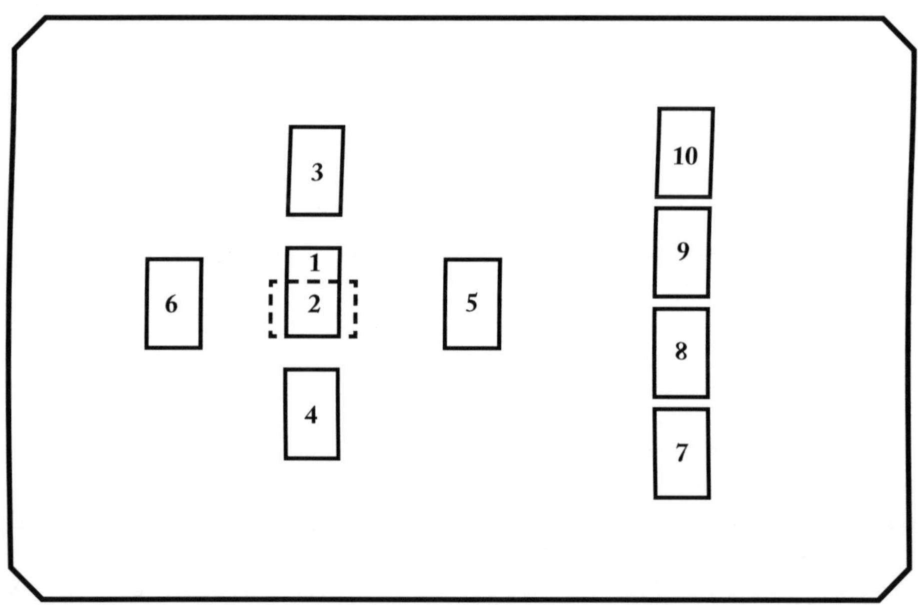

1: Current self

2: Crossing card (what is in tension with that self or your goals)

3: Crowning card (how the situation appears to you and others)

4: Base of the matter (underlying motivations, background)

5: Past influences, moving out of your life

6: Future influences, coming into your life

7: Near future self

8: How others see you, or your environmental influences

9: Hopes and/or fears (help draw together the rest of the reading)

10: Final outcome (for next little while, like six months)

There are so many ways to read tarot cards, as spreads or individually.[2] One way that people often suggest is to pull a daily card, experience it visually, viscerally, intellectually, or however you respond to it, and then read about it to add to your interpretation. This method familiarizes you with the more specific associations with the deck you're looking at as well as the broader themes across decks connected with a particular card.

2 See resources at the back of the book for examples of where to find more spread suggestions.

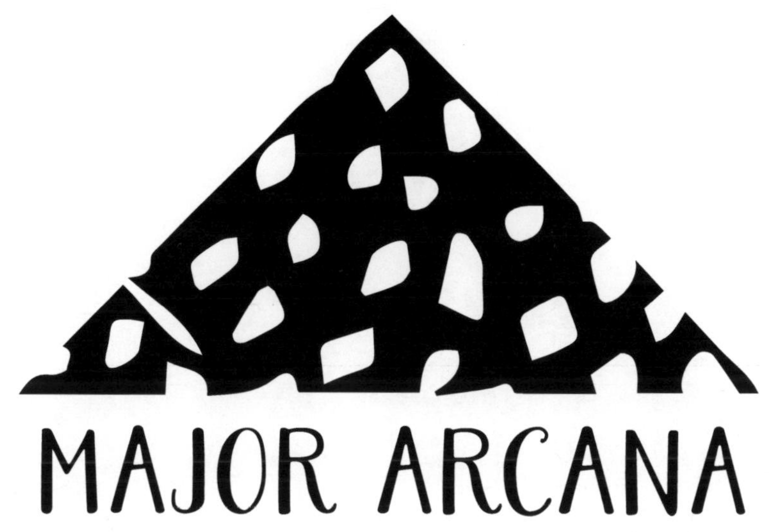

MAJOR ARCANA

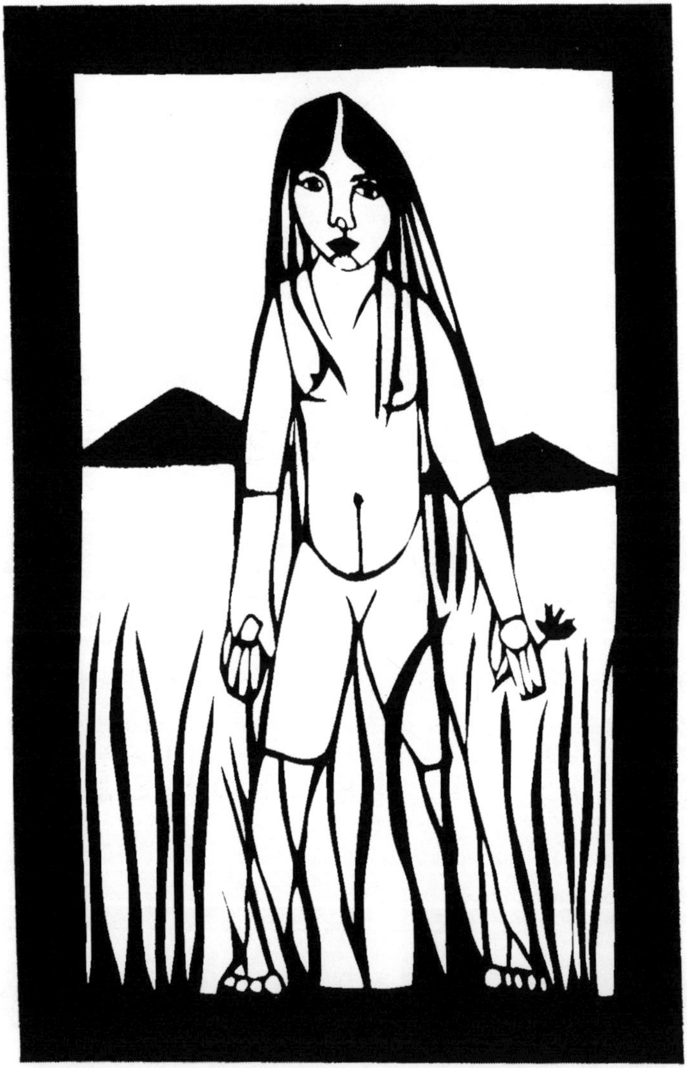

0. Innocence

new beginnings, change, excitement of fresh undertakings

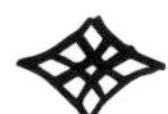

A child holds a flower and stands barefoot in tall grass, mountains of possibilities behind them. Perhaps they're foolish, but if they are it's only because they're open to everything, unbound by the artificial structures of job, school, family. They carry these structures as possibilities but don't rely on them, preferring to be excited about every option. Counting on fate and luck.

Innocence is full of all the possibilities with none of them realized, a true child or someone else who's societally assumed to have few of the qualities associated with adulthood (responsibility, restriction, direction)—wanderers, people who hear voices, tricksters. With this card, we find the clarity that many of us lack once we grow up and get ideas about what we should be doing versus what we feel moved to do.

This is a transformative card, emerging in a reading whenever you need spirit, action, and instinct to get through a difficult period. It appears in order to urge you to be optimistic and have faith in yourself, especially your internal animal self that may get downtrodden or forgotten by worldly expectations. You probably know what's best, on an instinctual, unplanned level, and it's probably a good time right now to leap into it, flower in hand, the road endless and inviting ahead.

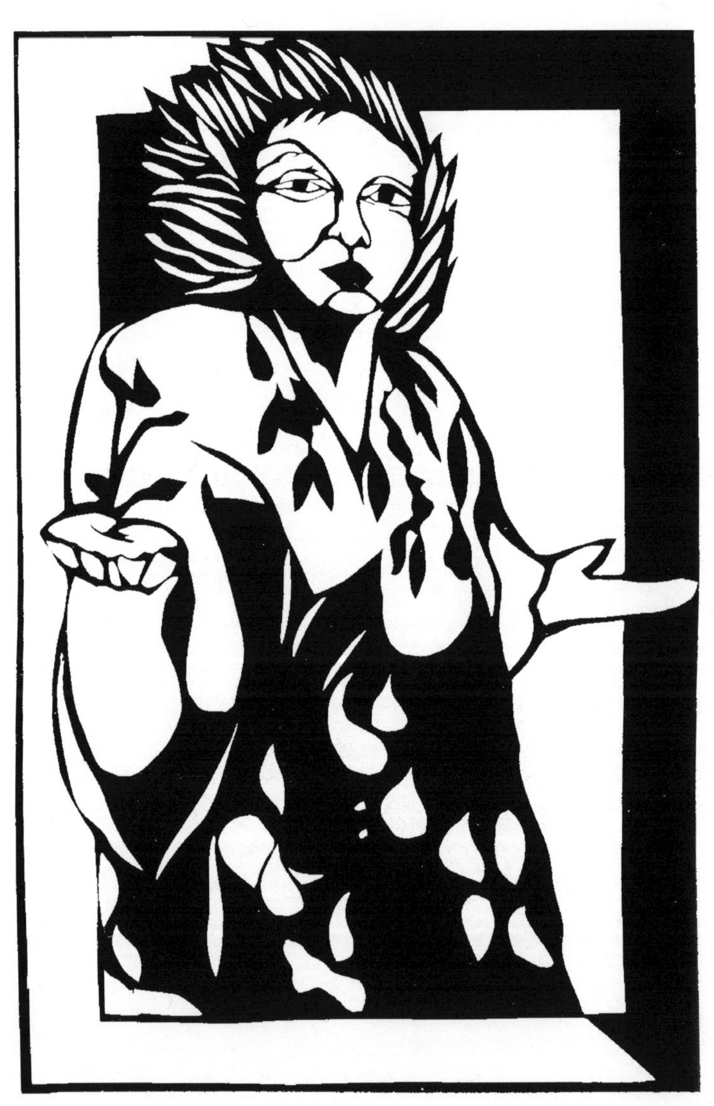

1. The Magician

sorceress, wisdom and common sense in daily life

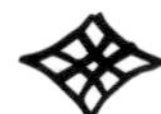

This woman is open to the world. Hands upturned, hair blowing, multiple patterns on her clothes—she is facing you, her eyes lined with age. She's doing it.

While her hands are open, her gaze is direct. The Magician represents the energy of the universe being grounded through you, a human. Implicit in this concept is that everyone has access to power and energy and magic, and the variables are only how they affect us, how we choose to access them, and what we do with them.

With this card, you're able to focus on and achieve your goals, create art, or otherwise contribute to life outside of yourself with energy that comes through you. Here you are—hands open, eyes focused, hair blowing, sleeves billowing, powerful.

In a reading, the Magician signifies your awareness of or ability to access this power. Maybe you're starting a new project or phase of life and can physically feel the energy inherent in this process. Maybe you're being affected by someone else's power, or you're figuring out the resources that are available to you and using them effectively for your contribution to the world. Ultimately, you're taking energy in, throwing it down in a directed and focused and wilful way, and knowing that whatever it becomes will exist outside of you.

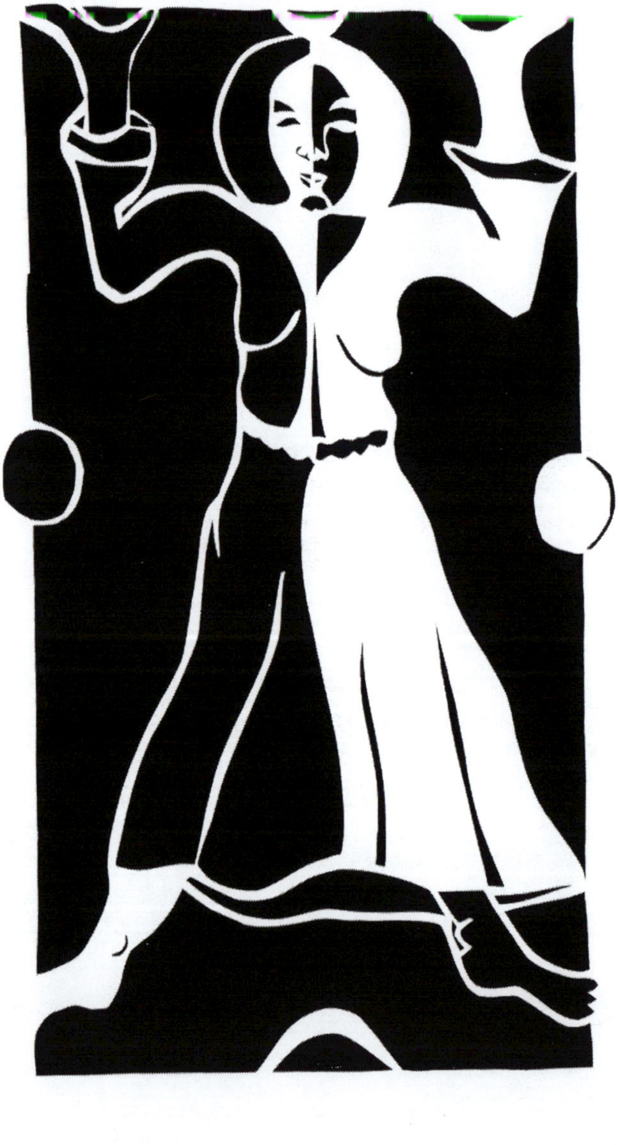

2. The Seer

priestess of hidden truths, meditative guardian, key

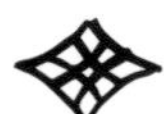

The person on this card holds up the sky, surrounded by the phases of the moon, split down the middle between black and white, a false duality that reminds us of the complementary nature of light and shade, colour, and in this case, the conscious and unconscious.

Here is someone who is connected with their internal world—perhaps psychic, definitely intuitive. Being connected with the mysterious feminine archetype and familiar with the larger forces beyond our control (like the moon) can indicate fear of the unknown but more likely the ability to draw on these forces, gaining knowledge and wisdom from non-rational, unconscious reflection.

The Seer can also indicate passivity, sometimes to the point of worldly withdrawal. This card can be a reminder that, when approached carefully, passivity gives the mind room to work and for inner wisdom to emerge. Once removed from the glare of external activity, we can access intuitive knowledge.

This card's appearance in a reading can signal your struggle with bringing this knowledge into consciousness, or getting caught up in internal processes to the point of inaction, fearing exposure and instead prioritizing the safety of internal life. On the other hand, it prompts you to draw on your intuition and wisdom, in order to recognize the false constructs of the external world and then to use this wisdom in a passionately engaged way.

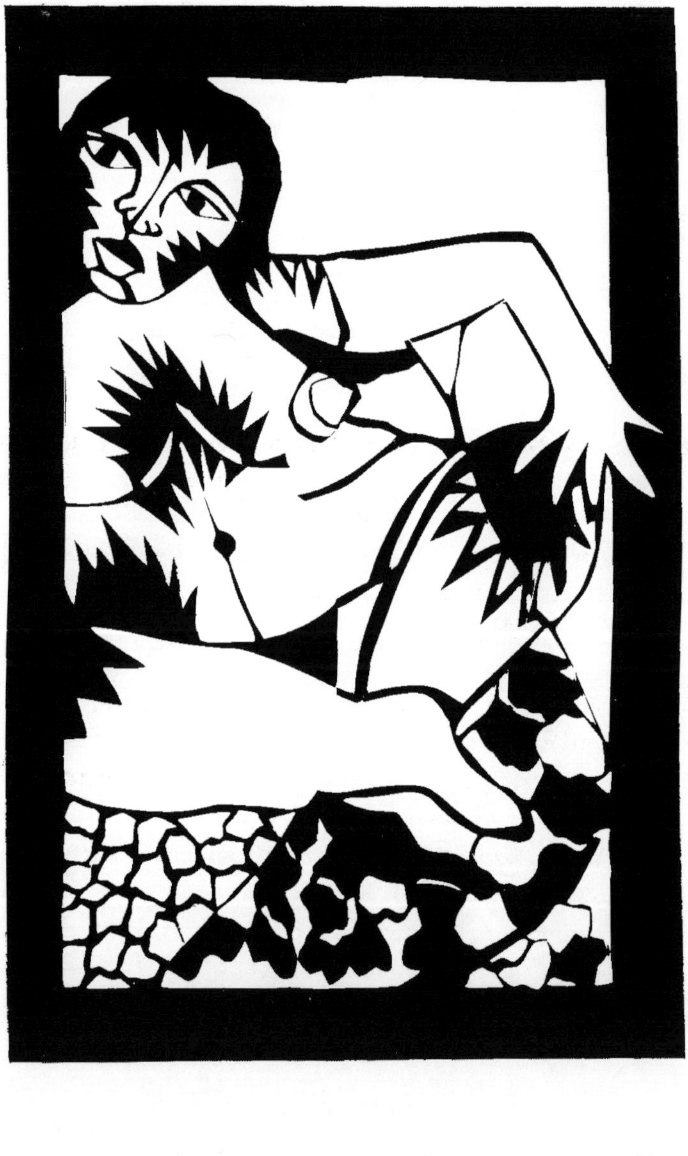

3. The Creator

nurturance, fertility, fruitful action, and development

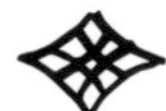

Their body marked with leaves or suns, maybe both, the Creator symbolizes the basis of life itself. They are naked, cross-legged, sort of in motion, on printed blankets or quilts. Comfort, receptiveness, sexuality, and creativity are this card's main associations.

The Creator appears at the beginning of the deck because it represents some of the foundational elements of life: nature, abundance, undifferentiated passion. If we come from histories or social contexts steeped in sexism or the devaluation of femininity, it can be helpful to think hard about receptiveness as a strong and positive characteristic. It could be healing to focus on the good in these qualities in your life now and see how much you can open up to them on your own terms.

In a reading, the Creator can remind you of a need for physical or sexual exploration or indulgence, for feeling without restraint, for being vulnerable in a real and substantial way. Depending on the situation, it may point to an excess of these elements and a need for some kind of self-control. But either way it reminds you of physical pleasure and natural profusion as basic and necessary to life. On a more mundane level, the Creator might indicate a time of literally reaping rewards, producing in abundance, receiving, or feeling in excess.

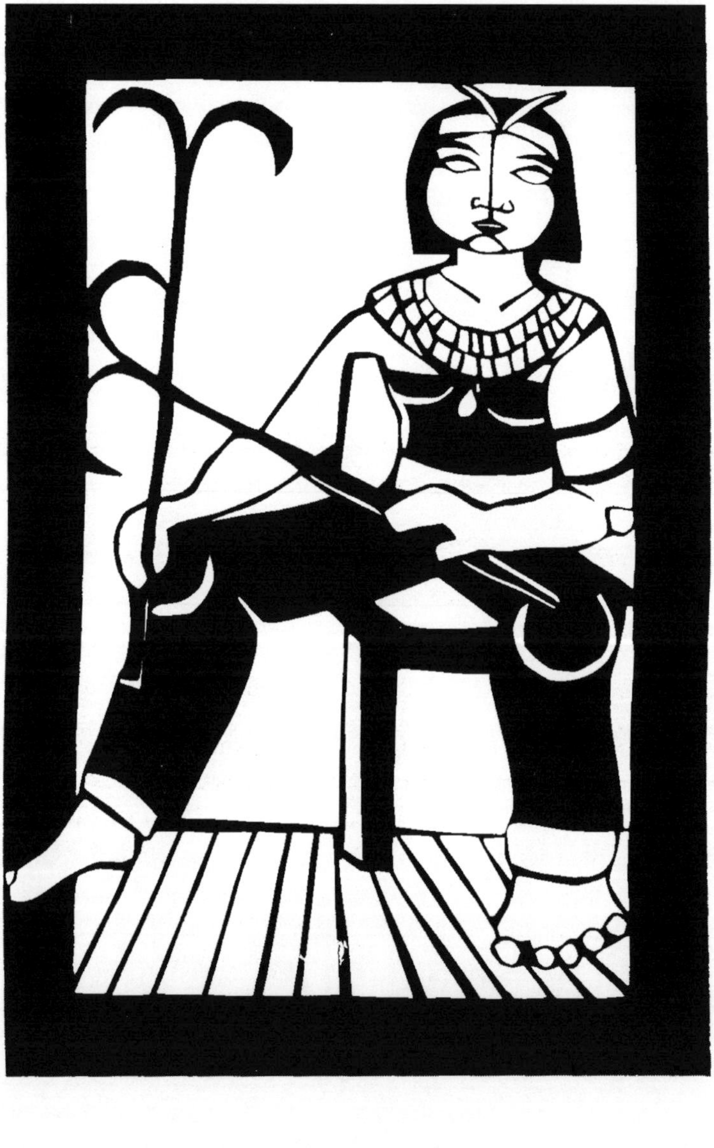

4. The Emperor

worldly power, Aries-like assertion, endurance, aggression

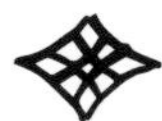

The figure on this card holds two instruments that could be rams' horns or iron pokers. Iron and rams are both associated with Aries, the astrological sign affiliated with this card, and therefore with achievement, breaking through, and beginnings based on testing the boundaries of any pre-existing structures encountered. The figure is also dressed in the fitted and coded pieces of somebody going into battle, another marker of the Emperor's aggression and enthusiasm: a tight torso piece, a burdensome collar, a headpiece with horns as well. They are barefoot and seated, but poised to leap up any minute.

The Emperor is the epitome of the phase of external achievement. This is a top, right here, in all the glory of rules and codes of behaviour (the foundations underlying growth, social belonging), and all of their drawbacks (overrestriction, stunted growth due to overriding power structures).

Rules and codes and power dynamics can be totally functional and hot and great, but a lot of them exist unquestioningly, even within our intimate relationships and subcultures. Sometimes the hardest and more rewarding response is each individual's, relationship's, and community's commitment to allowing for some structures and rejecting others—the ones that, in order to experience exhilaration in beginnings, need a semblance of a foundation or order from which to do so. Maybe as a gentle Daddy, or a mean Mommy.

If you get this card, you're being reminded on the one hand of the authority figures in your life, about your authority over your own life, and whether either has too little or too much of a hold on you. If you're overly self-restrictive, or if you're being constrained to the point of withering by an external powerful figure, consider doing whatever is in your power to shift that. Either way you'll end up with a few hard-won internal rules.

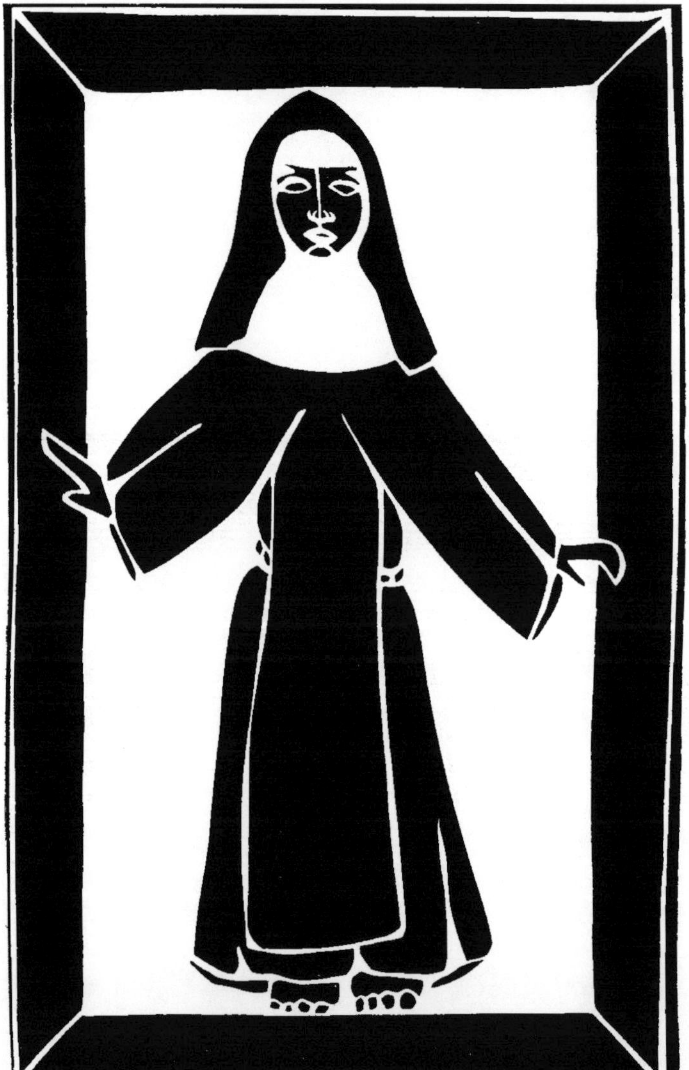

5. The Hierophant

holder of formal religion, legalistic institutions

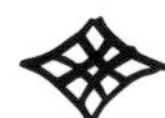

Robed and standing, authoritative and firm, this instructor reaches out to the edges of the card's frame.

As a medium between humans and gods, the Hierophant can draw your attention to formal institutions or cultural matrices in your life—be they heavy and archaic and imposed or more consciously developed collections or revisions of those that you use in your own internal scaffolding.

The inherent tension is between being manipulated by or thoughtlessly succumbing to the structures of cultural establishments (maybe you think cops are great, or that a PhD will provide you with self-worth) versus what elements of these same structures can actually serve someone or some purpose (doing your taxes to get some money, or tutoring kids in an otherwise hostile school system).

Where this card is found in a reading is where you'll find your own sense of inner obedience verging on conformity. Ideally the balance will tilt toward inner stability premised on your useful scraps of the culture that surrounds you rather than a wholehearted internalization of its totality.

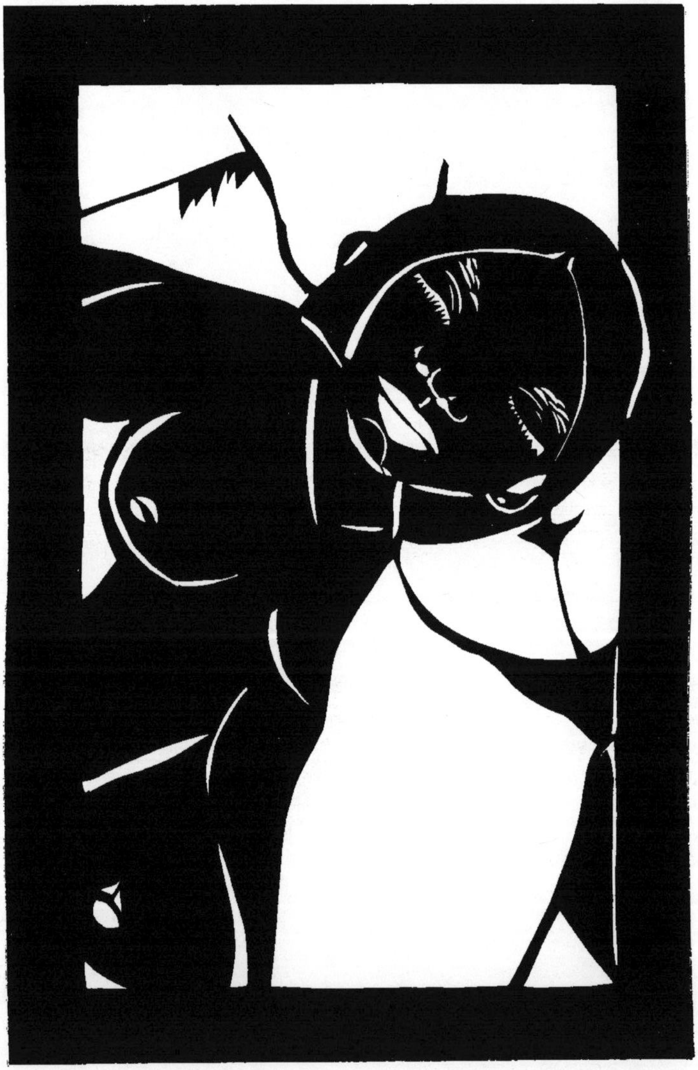

6. The Lovers

love, beauty, attraction and affection, erotic/caring relationships

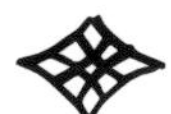

This close-up of two nearly naked women, spent, suggests that wash of post-coital exhaustion that can be so relaxing and so covered in sweat. Or else maybe these two are just having a nice moment together, comfortable being near each other, sated and loving.

Celebrating love, sexual and otherwise, is part of what this card asks you to do. It also wants you to seek unity with others, and to confirm that the choices you are making are rooted in motivations of both your head and heart, but encourages you to pursue the ones that foreground passion. Furthermore, it can point to breaking isolation through relationships, to a level where you find meaning beyond the self because you've gone beyond yourself.

The other unity and relationship it urges you to attend to is that within yourself, to find peace or compromise—to break the constraints of your ego and combine it with the physical, uniting passion and reason in a whole.

The Lovers can therefore turn up in a reading to indicate this kind of unifying of the self, support from a lover, or simply a valuable or significant relationship. It can also reveal your overriding nostalgia for a lost love, and urge you to once again take risks, be vulnerable—the usual queer directives. Finally, it reminds you to take ownership of and responsibility for the choices you've made, rational, passionate, risky, restrained, and all.

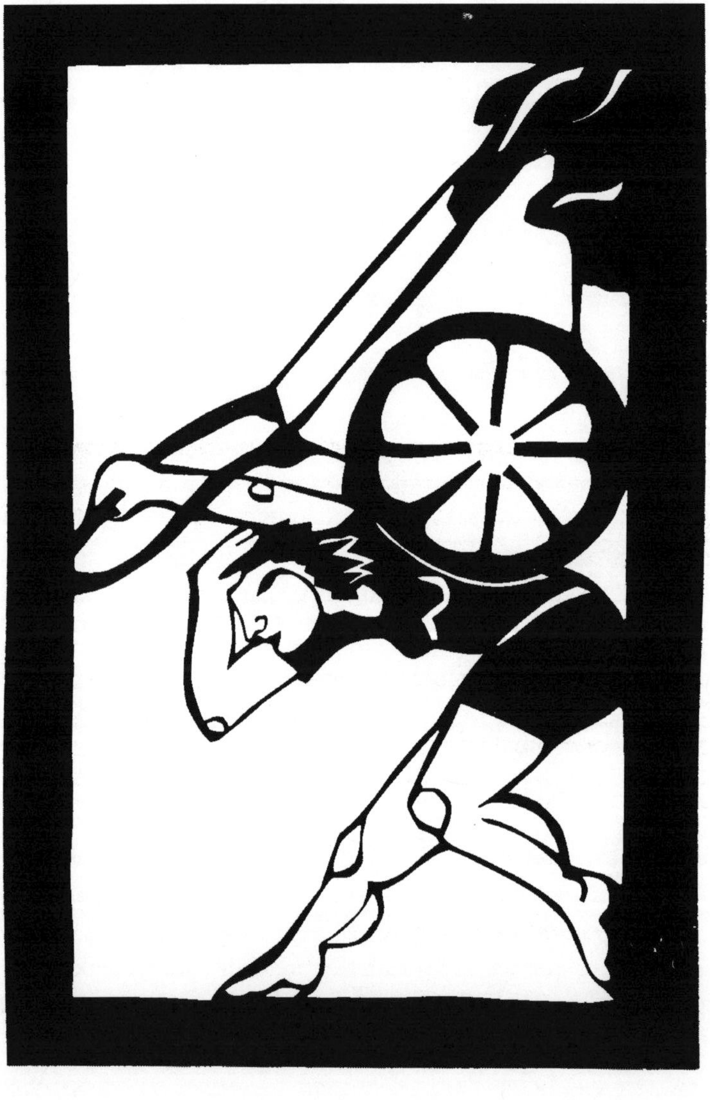

7. The Chariot

conquest, intelligence, balance through work, dexterity

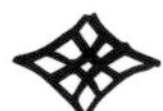

Here is someone taking on the external world through sheer force of will. Look at those calf muscles! Look at how only one arm is being used to haul a giant machine on the back! Look at that determined face and the flying hair!

Physical competence is one possible reading for this card, but certainly not the only one. While strength may be easiest to illustrate in that context, the Chariot really refers to the application of willpower to whatever an individual chooses, and achieving one's aims in a public and applauded way.

At its best, the Chariot does not use brute force but instead negotiates (or even compromises) with the elements employed en route to its shining destination. Emotion, creativity, intelligence, and strength are harnessed but ideally given some level of free rein as well, so that even while subbing they are in consensual relationship with you, the driver.

This card carries a lot of meanings in readings, but the potential for victory is there, underpinned by inner struggle or self-discipline in the face of indulgence. Torn parts of yourself may be corralled into working together; you might consider examining them in case they are ready to explode apart and further shatter you. Your powerful will is doing great things for you, and you could afford to be modest about or aware of the cycles of achievement and lack, enthusiasm and depression. Here they come, here you go.

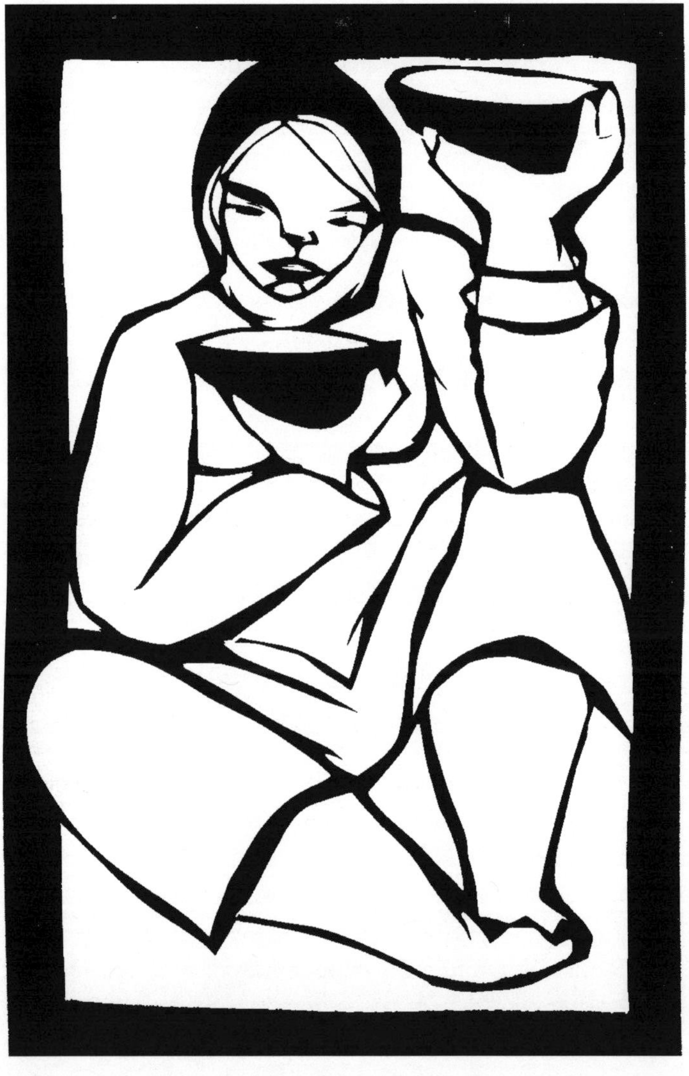

8. Justice

cosmic balance, equity, maintenance of equilibrium

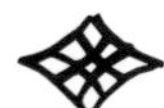

Draped in a long garment, her face downturned, this person concentrates on balancing two bowls in her hands. These are the scales, and let's not think of them as a corrupt justice system but rather as our human ability to find internal truths, take responsibility for our actions and histories, and actively move forward carrying the knowledge rooted in and emerging from these experiences.

While in certain ways this is an inward-turning card, it is not a passive one. These characteristics are often confused, but movement—as it turns out—is not the same as action. Restless outer-world involvement comes before this card in the Major Arcana, and here you are asked to turn inward to find the source of what your actions should be, to test the limits of your free will, and to seek justice in a real way. The first step of this process is often one of introspection, self-analysis, checking yourself, whatever.

In a reading, this card asks you to be honest with and accountable to yourself and others. To make art for real. To start restructuring the non-profit that you work for that actually has the shittiest labour practices. To think about how, though the other parties were responsible too, you were partially responsible—inasmuch as you did have input and control—for the conditions that led to your breakup, your intolerable living situation, your tepid family dynamics. With this card you're not allowed to gloss over things or put up a front. It can imply that events have played out as they should have, and you have the substantial task of trusting that and acting suitably, first by feeling out what is motivating and troubling you, and then by effectively changing the world around you based on this reflection.

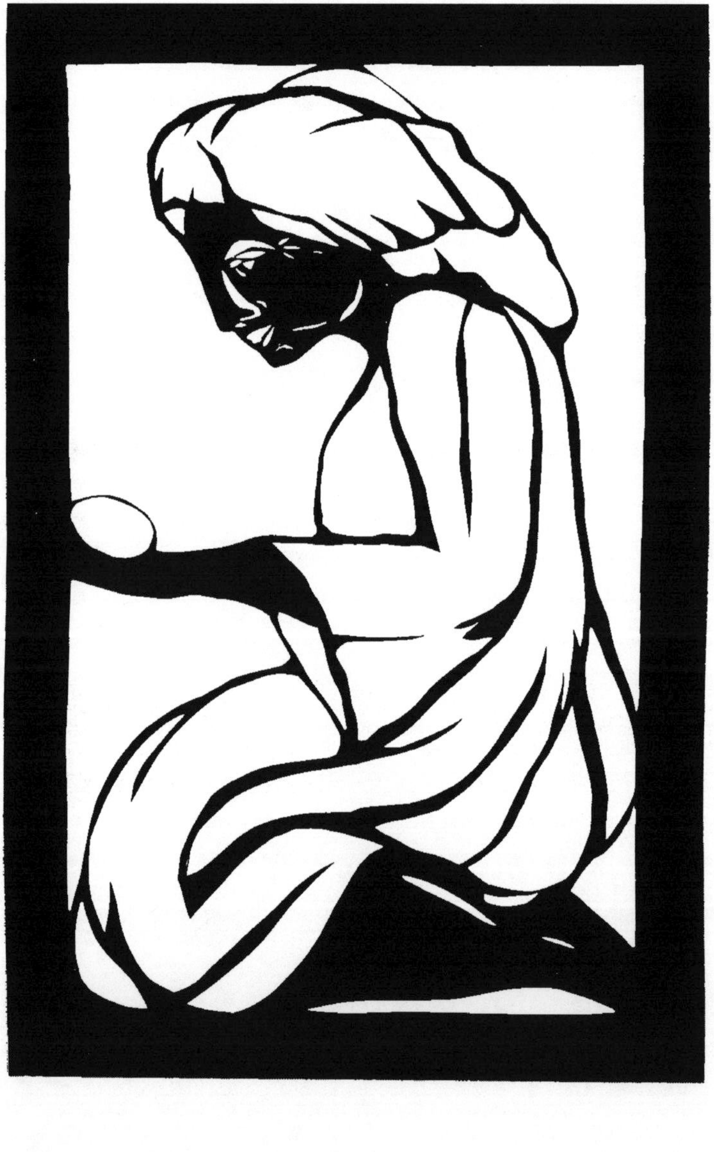

9. The Hermit

introspective, reflective, ascetic, inward search for knowledge

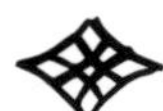

A lined, thoughtful profile gazes into a stone being held by the figure on this card. Her head and body are wrapped loosely and she is kneeling, presumably thinking, assessing, or divining.

The Hermit highlights the necessity of withdrawal or at least introspection for the purpose of self-awareness. She represents individual learning or mentorship as opposed to institutional instruction, dogma, or god. This is someone, found in yourself or in someone more experienced than you, who teaches you about yourself and your connection to the world by briefly removing you from the concerns of the outer world to examine a plain piece of it, like that rock in her hands.

If you get this card in a reading, it may be time to look inward, perhaps to go somewhere quiet and unpopulated. A therapist or some other kind of guide could be useful for you right now, or possibly you are acting in that role for other people. Overall, it calls for a serious approach to inner needs, with the understanding that this process necessarily precedes liberation.

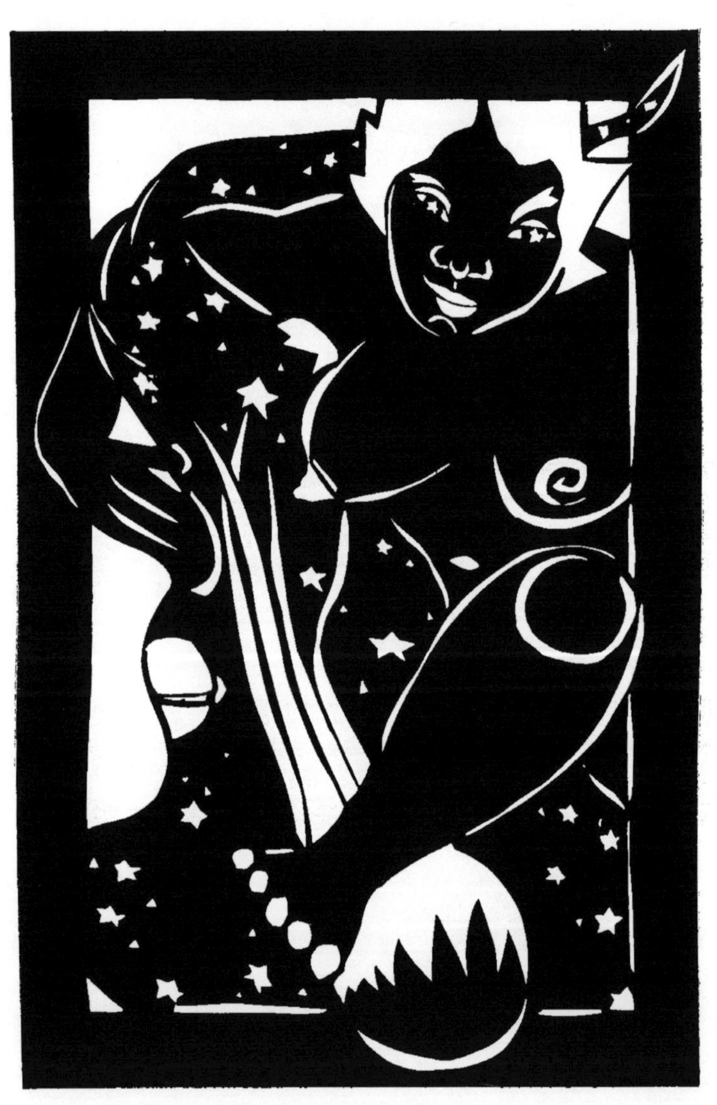

10. The Comet

good fortune through change, felicity, destiny

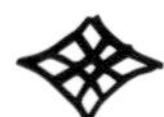

This person is covered in stars, spirals on her nipples and more stars in her eyes. A comet shoots down behind her foot and maybe that's the Milky Way draped around her body. Saturn, ruler of conscious choice and discipline, is behind her. She's watching the comet burn her foot, knowing it's a pain she cannot control.

In most decks, no human figure appears on this card because it specifically asks you to think of life and its patterns as existing beyond the confines of this particular existence. With karmic connotations, it directs you toward considering how you unconsciously invite your current circumstances, allowing you to take responsibility for whatever influence you have had on them. But it also allows for the elements of life you don't have control over, and pushes you to adapt to them. They are there, and you are living with them, regardless of whether you invited them in or not.

In a reading, the Comet suggests a change of circumstances or fate, seemingly beyond your conscious control. Often these changes consist of a reversal of fortune toward the good, but because implicit in the card lies the prompt to understand the cycles of life in a truly holistic way, they may also feel bad or hard. In any case, it asks you to prepare yourself for change, be adaptable, and accept the role you play as well as the elements over which you don't have control.

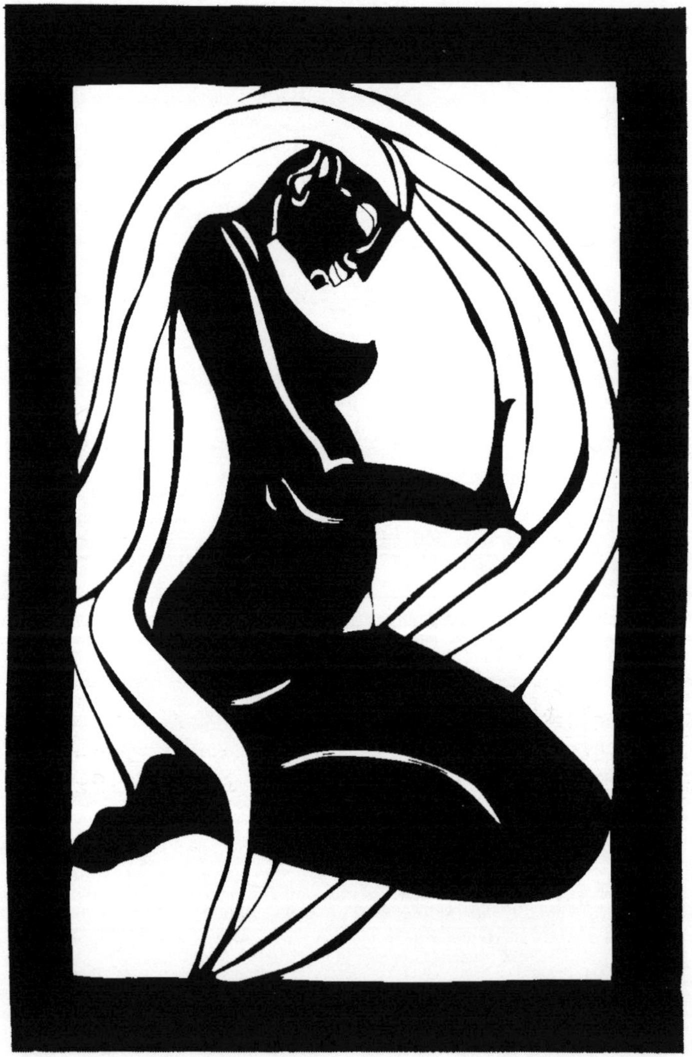

11. Strength

sexual energy, sensual and life power, courage

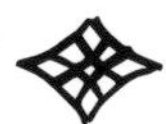

A woman gazes at her upturned breasts as her hair flows around her entire kneeling body. She is relaxed, but clearly aroused or at least energized. She is working with her multidirectional hair to shape it and appreciate it, without letting it entirely impede her movement or her wishes.

The second, more inward-focused segment of the Major Arcana, of which Strength is a part, signals that you are intentionally mastering life. You turn within and see how you're doing there, and Strength works to direct or make sense of the chaos of impulses you might find inside. If you are someone who thinks that you can consciously manage your emotional responses, this card gives you a greater ability to do so.

However, more subtly, it signifies a relationship forged between your emotional and rational lives, which are in flux and in productive conflict with each other. This conflict will slowly create the rumblings of a self that, while perhaps disparate, is at least in a process of internal negotiation of a satisfying and even beautiful outcome.

Strength, in a reading, shows where you are in a transformative relationship with your basic self, where you're letting go of control and relying on negotiation and trust. There is a taming connotation to this card, but my preferred reading is one of collaboration between animal and human, hair and brain, child and adult—so that all parts are heard and respected, as equals.

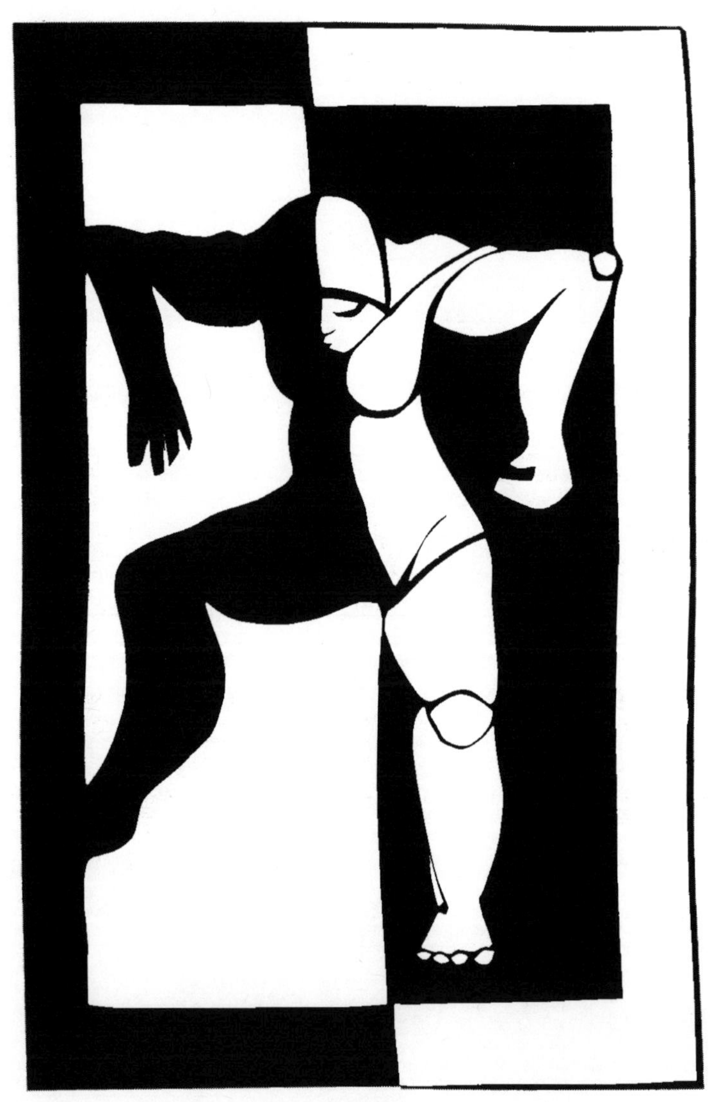

12. Art

transformation, creative cosmic change, inner hope

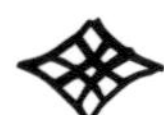

In this deck, the figure's head in Art is unexpectedly at the top of the card (most decks picture someone hanging from their ankles), but her body is split between contrasting shades. She's looking down, elbows and one knee pulled upward by invisible string, wearing a bathing suit and a little cap.

This swimsuit imagery may point to the water aspect of this card—surrender to intuition and emotion in opposition to force of will. The split lighting connotes semiwithdrawal from the world, an internal concession for the sake of future action. Art tells you to let go so that you can keep going, if you know what I mean.

If you get this card in a reading, your independence is being highlighted. You might be stubbornly resisting social pressure, or fighting yourself, or doing something that feels right for some inexplicable reason and even though others would disagree with your actions. It asks you to think about the exchange of loss for a gain, settle into peace after difficulty, and grow from experience. You might have to release your will to allow things to happen, and your situation may reverse quite soon. Art calls for faith, but also compromise. It calls for surrender.

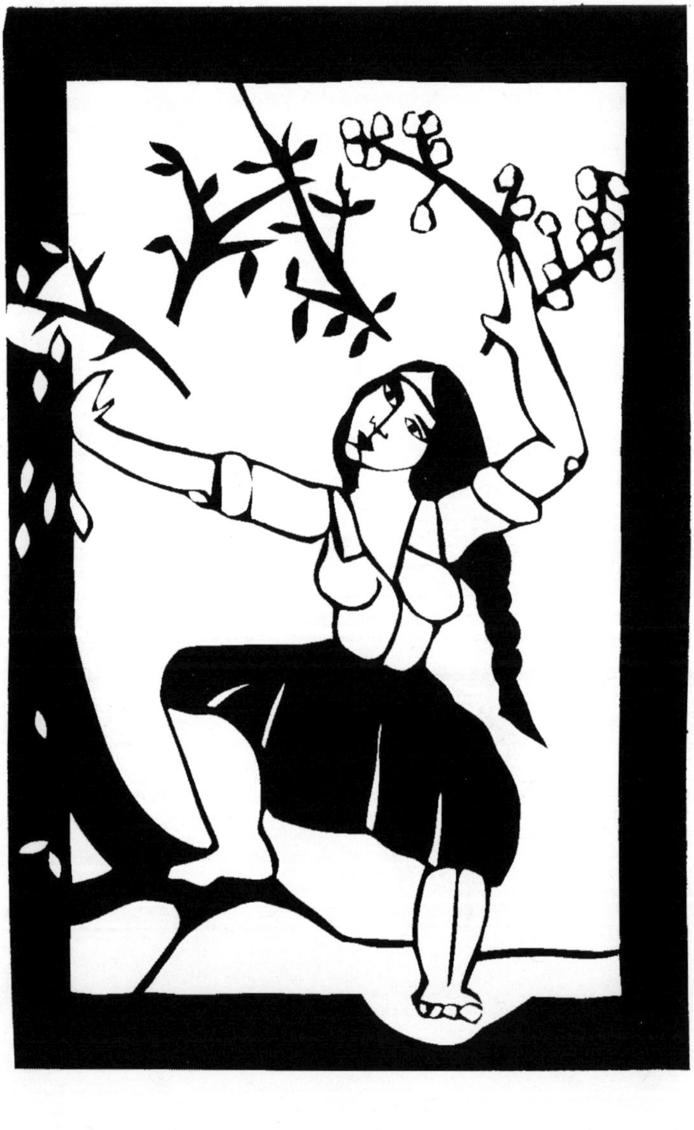

13. The Juggler

darkness, forward motion from one realm to another, death/rebirth

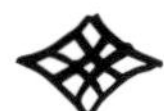

Playing with branches in different phases of bloom, the Juggler handles the seasons. She is dancing, her braid swinging, alert to the cycle being instigated by her movement.

The Juggler is primarily about movement—specifically, about the moment of transformation in a movement phase, when old patterns have been shed and a new level of consciousness reached. Of course, this description can include physical death, but it more likely points to profound transformation, the moment of change after a period of mourning and contemplation.

It likely represents a death of the ego. With extreme change in patterns, your old self may no longer be recognizable to you. You've stopped obsessing over that old relationship, that job that defined you, that place you lived. Now there's a huge amount of room for your new life to flood in and take over.

If, in a reading, this card is reversed or if it's not speaking to you, it's perhaps because your fears of death are deeper than you imagine. Boredom, inertia, and stagnancy are also qualities of this card, and they are often tied to an internal struggle between letting go and fearing change or death. Regardless of your level of resistance, when you do pull the Juggler, the change has probably already taken place on most levels. Now the shift is here, ready to drain you, pull apart your foundations, and pour in what is new and useful and potentially unrecognizably you.

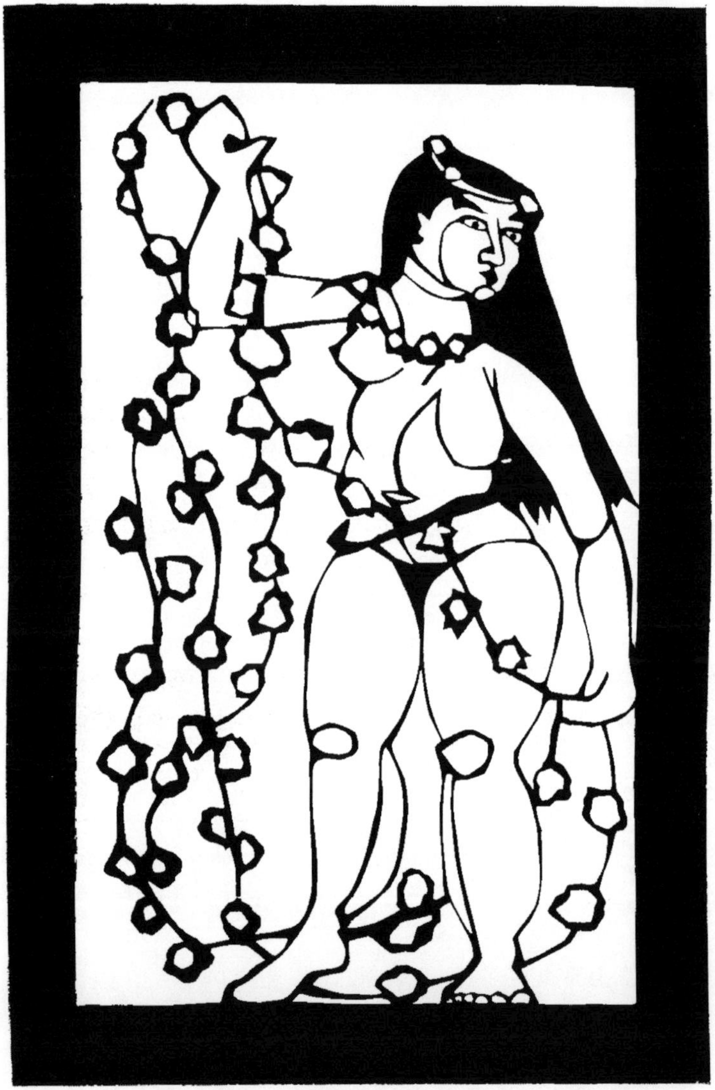

14. Grace

healer, supporter, holistic nurturer, revitalization

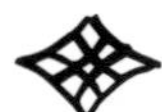

Grace in this deck involves the careful untangling of a long string of lights or flowers. The figure is clearly focused on the final end of the string, after having worked through the mess. On a more metaphoric level, Grace is associated with death, conflicts, or imbalance and extremes, and more importantly the ability, as this person has, to work through them with care and without haste.

Grace calls for self-control, not through socially internalized suppression and compartmentalization but through appropriate and thoughtful responses to all situations. It asks for compromise, harmony, and moderation. Specifically, it suggests you bring together the divergent elements of your life and, using intuitive guidance, blend them together in a way that allows for harmony and healing. It also shows the growth that has occurred since you experienced a trying situation. You've moved through grief and conflict, and now you're able to more deeply balance your life.

It might be boring not to go to extremes, but where this card emerges in a reading requires that you do just that. It asks you to slow down, loosen the unnecessary barriers between your family, work, lovers, and others, and approach difficult situations calmly.

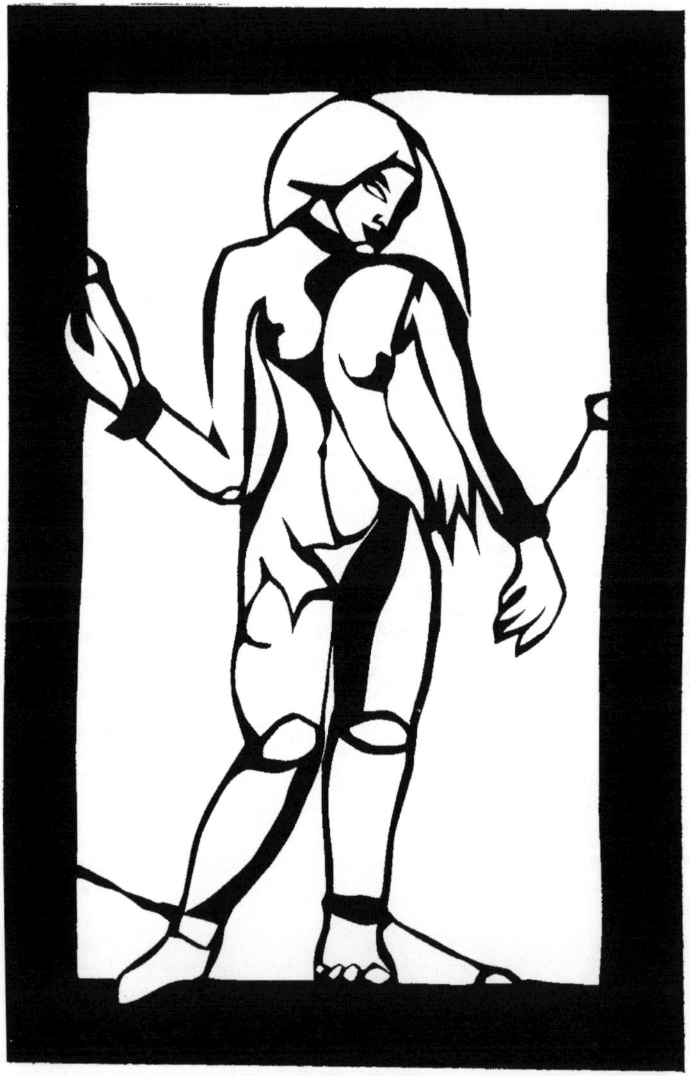

15. Oppression

violence, negative sexual energy, aggression

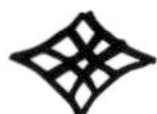

Wrists and ankles bound to thin chains, this person stands naked. She gazes at the clamp around one of her wrists, her body fluid and relaxed. She is not trying to get out. In most decks this card is called the Devil, and it represents something that might look like oppression but could also be complicated by the way oppression interacts with self-imposed limitations. As demonstrated in this image, Oppression offers the possibility for escape from literal restraints, but the figures involved are too consumed or destroyed by the fact of constraint to think of leaving.

The tension here is between indulgence, attachment, wanting everything; and restraint, discipline, and inner needs. Call it puritan, call it capitalist, but the symbolism likely predates those frameworks. It reveals the self-destruction brought about by an excess of external striving, and points to the possibility of self-awareness through facing the messy, needy, obsessive parts of the self with care and discipline in order to grow.

There may be some room in this card for simultaneously working within the harder-to-bend scaffolding of structural oppression, in which power is working from every angle to devitalize or dehumanize you, and thinking of the smaller-scale ways that you are involved in doing that to yourself. Further, Oppression opens up the possibility for self-release, with the help of clear judgment. These qualities are likely to aid in extracting yourself from whatever dissatisfying bondage you've trained yourself into.

When you get this card in a reading, consider drawing on this intentionality to support your grappling against whatever trapped, lifeless power struggles or crushing burdens you are in or under—your desire to fit into socially sanctioned relationship models, your soul-trampling but simultaneously caring family dynamics—and releasing shame. Liberation from constraints will come when all involved do this kind of work.

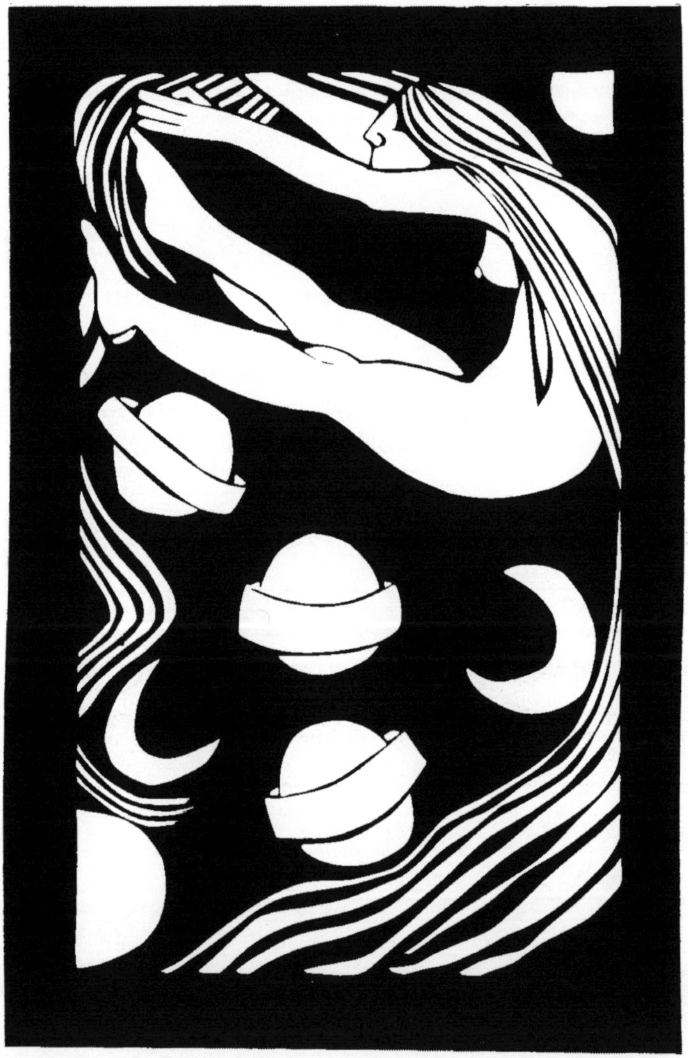

16. The Tower

momentous worldly change, either personal or political

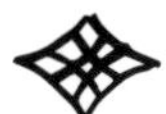

The figure on this card is flipping through the universe, being blown through the unknown, backwards, her hair sweeping around the planets that surround her. Big changes are taking place or are about to happen, and all she can do is ride with them. She hasn't brought any clothes with her; she can't see where she's going; she seems to have entirely left the earth.

This card calls for a revision of structures, sometimes intentional but usually seemingly external. Often what happens in Tower situations is that you'll push circumstances so far that they'll fly apart beneath you; another possibility is that they'll collapse or crisis will occur in response to something you've done, but as a reminder that human structures are inherently unstable. Your relationships can be blown into the ether. Your money can disappear or be used all at once. Your home can deteriorate. Your body can shift beyond your previous conscious understanding of its structure and function.

And mainly what you can do is roll with it. Let things fall apart so that everything will be a zillion times better and more free and whole afterward. That work can be onerous and can feel downright impossible. But fighting against it might extend the feeling that everything is precarious and has been for a while—there's always that chance more things are going to get rumpled up in order for the pain to release new growth.

This card in a reading reminds you of where your restless trapped unconscious is destroying its cage, clambering out until you've caught up with what—in the aftermath—can be revelatory or amazing.

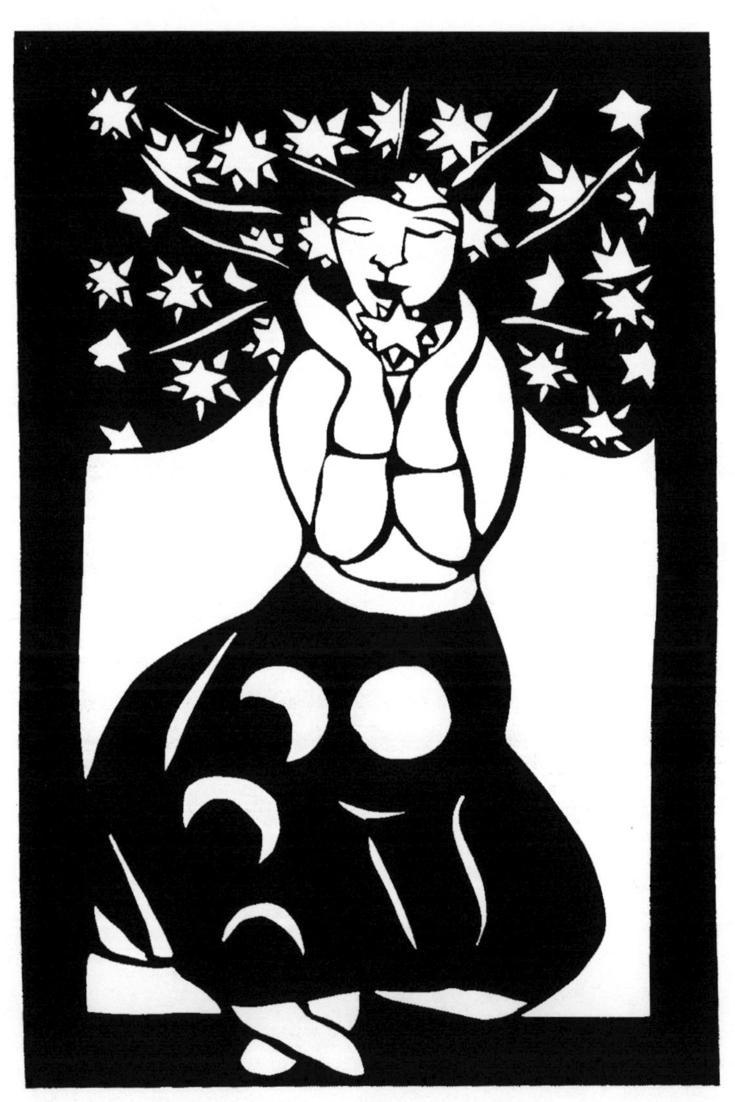

17. The Star

hope, realized visions, bright prospects, dreaminess

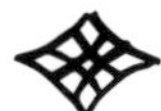

Her giant hair full of stars as well as a star against her lip, eyes closed, the Star is seated with the phases of the moon on her skirt. Her mouth is mildly content. She is sitting still, doing little, relieved and washed clean after what was frankly a crisis.

Implicit in the chaos and destruction of the Tower, which precedes this card, is the Star. Here is the emptied-out, extreme calm after a time of turmoil and distress. This card represents the beginning of the next phase, drained of distractions, conscious of oppression but for a moment washed of its weight.

The Star is restorative. When self-doubt and external circumstances collaborate to drain you and your community of the ability to support each other and fight, this card suggests a moment in the beginning of its renewal. Bringing down the structures that undermine us is a legitimate and necessary goal, but we wouldn't be able to begin that work without the meanings assigned to this card: hope, trust, calm, meditative release.

When this card appears in a spread, circumstances have begun to improve. This is a post-disaster hope, one not sought through conscious direction but by the full and heavy surrender of grief and loss. After having experienced those extremes, we are able to continue to live without the Star. Here you are calm, beginning to be restored, and able to trust in some internal vision that will bring you back into the world, changed but not broken past the point of renewal.

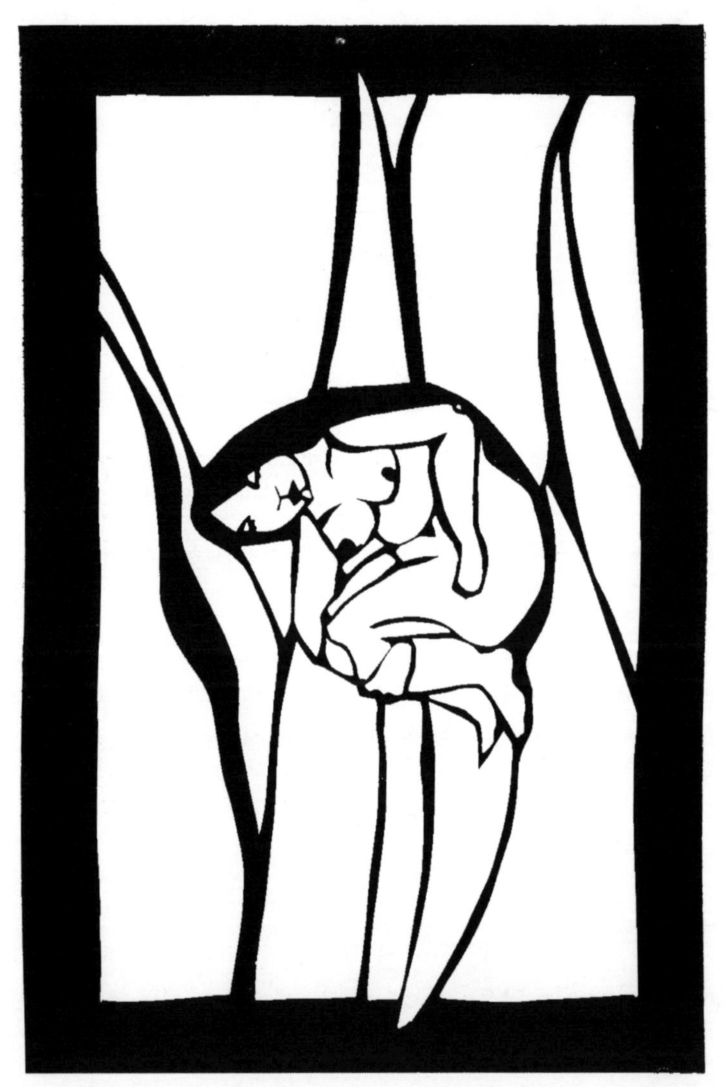

18. The Moon

intuitive feeling, spiritual growth, woman-centred strength

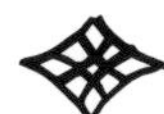

On the Moon card, someone rides on water. Actually, it could be hills or fields, or maybe the moon itself? What's clear is that it's not clear, and that is one of the overwhelming associations with the Moon—the half-lit, hazy possibilities that leave you fearful, confused, or disturbed.

There is power in those possibilities—the Moon also indicates psychic awakening, or being in touch with the darker, messier parts of yourself that are lost in full sunlight. It coaxes you into retreat, in order to sit with that intuitive sludge emerging, pay attention to dreams, and ride your emotional waves.

Getting this card in a reading means that you currently have more access than usual to creativity and intuition. It pleads with you not to fight whatever's waking up in you, or trying to crawl out—because increased intuition can also bring disturbing dreams, confusion, and basic psychic fears, and fighting such things can increase them. Here you are, just riding them, be they water or fields or moonscape, feeling the bumps under your butt and finding out where you'll emerge, more conscious and complete.

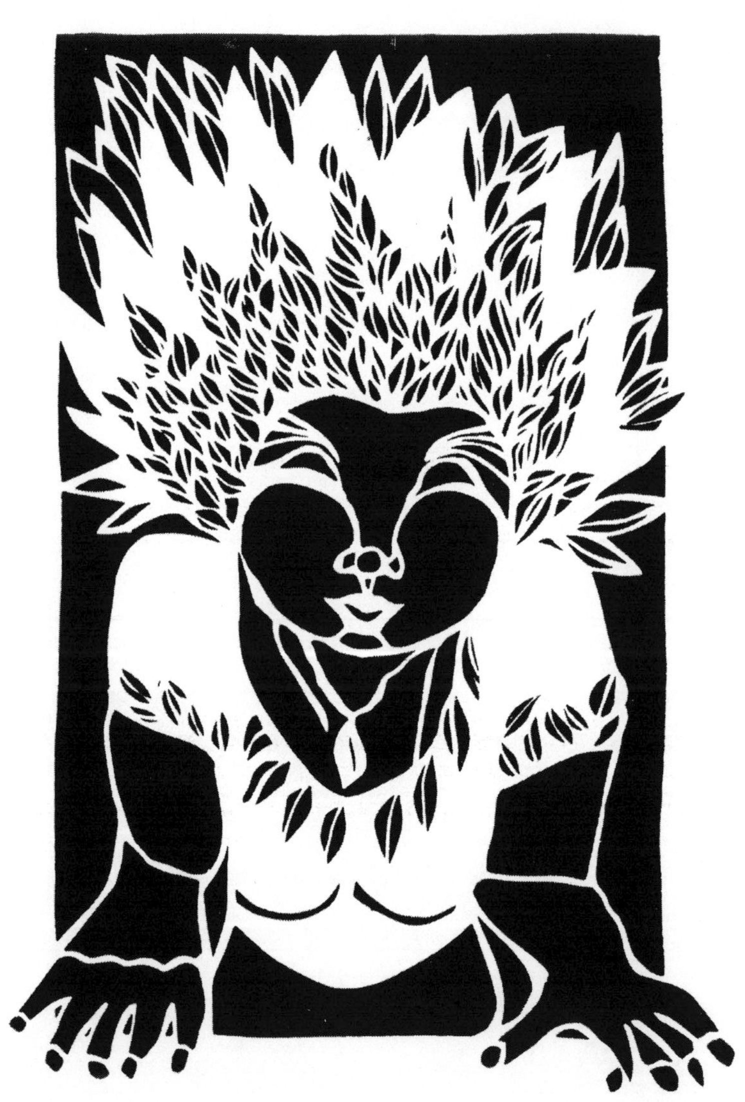

19. The Sun

triumph, healing, growth, health, optimism

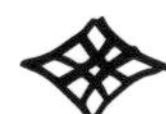

This card shows a blissful figure, cheeks gathered up around the eyes in joy, leaning forward eagerly, hair radiating around her face, manner radiating the qualities of uninhibited childhood. This person also has beautiful nails—an externalization of a portion of the wearer's inner truth: her beauty salient, her self cared for.

The Sun connects your inner and outer worlds so that, like the person in this image, you are beaming from within, beautifully adorned without. It is also connected with beginnings, like the emergence of spring, as the sun itself reasserts its presence after the crush of winter. It exhibits happiness, the easy joy that comes with connecting feelings and actions, yourself, and the universe.

Like the figure on this card whose hair is the fire of the sun, spring, and enthusiasm, when you pull this card in a reading you are overjoyed and ready to push forward into a life that will surely be more exciting or at least motion filled than it has been for a while. Everything is alive, and everything is beautiful, and this could be really annoying for anyone else around you who isn't feeling it, but you are, so hopefully they let you enjoy it. It's part of a cycle, and they'll get there too.

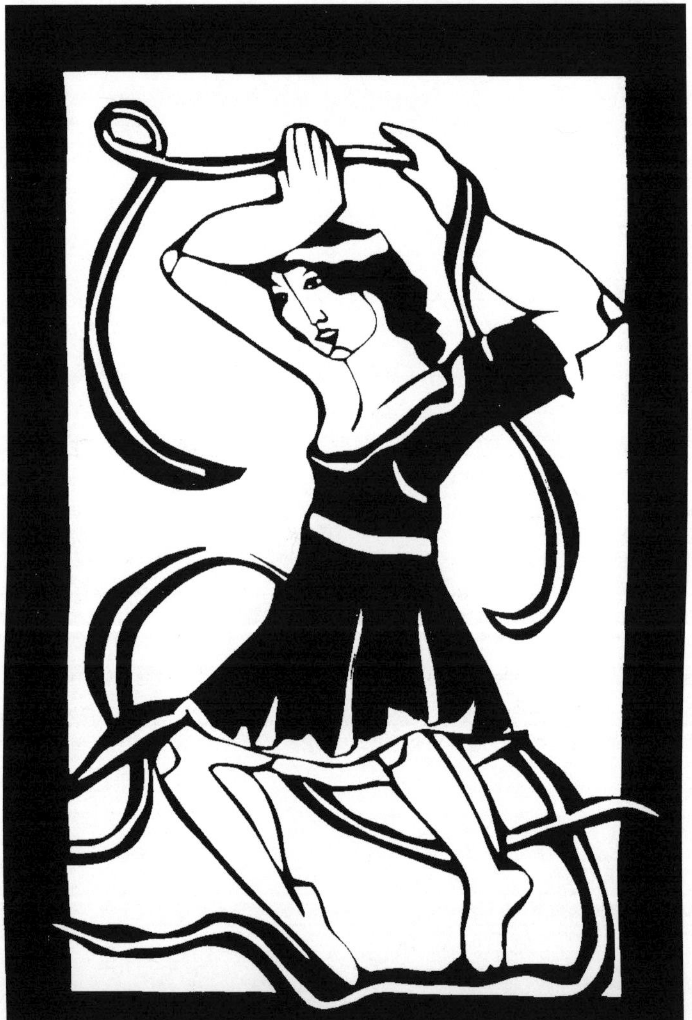

20. Rebirth

creative fullness, glad tidings, artistic invention

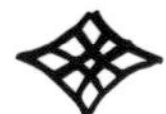

Dancing with ribbons, wearing a one-sleeved dress, and tripping around with her arms above her head, this person is overjoyed to be beginning again. The second to last in the Major Arcana, this card points to a summing up of experience.

But during that dance, or maybe before it, there's some serious thinking to do. Before going through a full transformation, or rebirth, a person is moved to reflect on and evaluate past actions and inactions, mistakes and good choices—all in order to go forward into wholeness and honesty with themself.

You may be feeling an internal drive to be honest with yourself and value the work you've done within the constraints of your external circumstances. The alternative to assigning value to this change is occasionally self-pity and blaming others, which Rebirth warns against. Because while your circumstances may be lousy, you still have agency over how you reflect on them, use your experiences, and shape your next phase of life. This card proposes heavy reflection, because here you are at the end of an era.

Furthermore, it's already happening. Even if you are struggling, procrastinating, regretting old decisions, Rebirth tells you that whatever it was you were doing/feeling/thinking before, it's over. You're facing all the bullshit and romance and work of your past, looking at where it's brought you, and dealing with that, whatever it is.

When you get this card in a reading, it is a time of rewards, integration and wholeness, and self-liberation, which Rebirth also connects inextricably to the liberation of all. Move forward, and say goodbye to what you used to be, because here you are now, changed, dancing with ribbons.

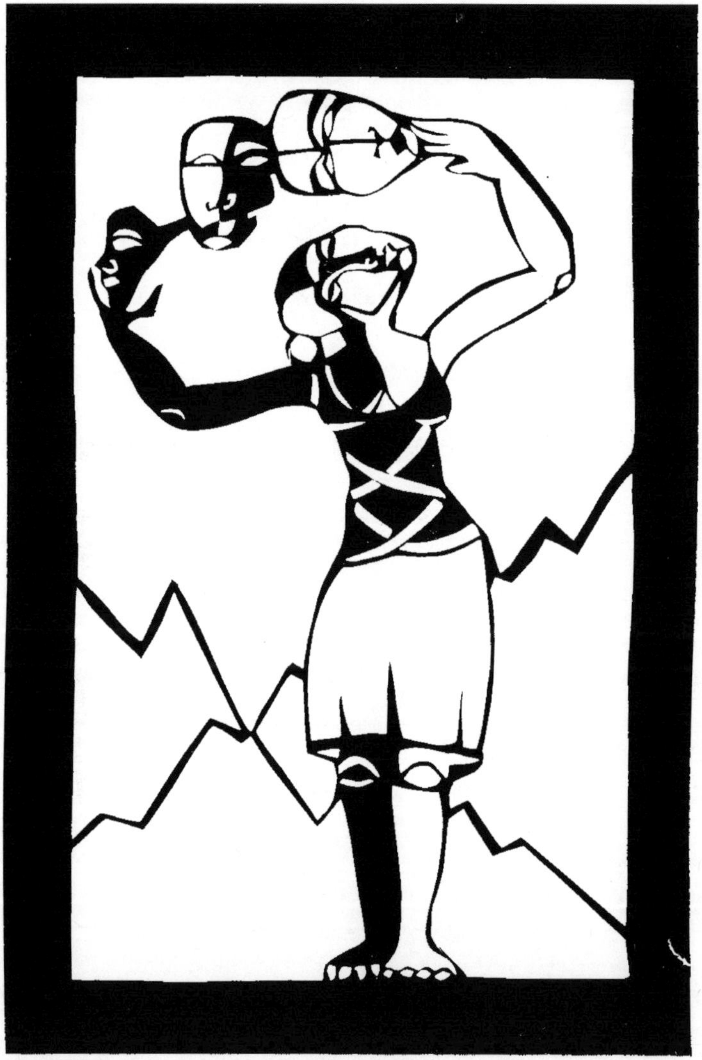

21. The World

completion, culmination, joyous action

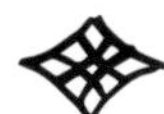

This person is gently floating a number of masks above their head, grounded and unruffled about the collection, not needing to wear them but recognizing that they are parts of their current whole self. This guy is truly complete, balancing their selves gently and perfectly.

This is the final card of the Major Arcana—having struggled through outer-world problems, self-analysis, and finally the breakdown of the ego, you've culled everything from that journey and found yourself here, whole. You've wrestled all your inner and outer selves into a coherent but unrepressed union, alongside the universe and the collective unconscious.

It also indicates completion of a cycle, with the implicit suggestion that a new one will begin immediately, but that this particular one has reached its perfect culmination. Underlying this achievement are difficult lessons, ones that have hopefully been assimilated through discipline and delay in order that your next cycle will have a new focus.

The World, on some level, is absolute fulfilment. In a reading, depending on its position, it could be something more mundane, like finishing whatever project you're working on, but symbolically and broadly it aims to depict enlightenment and wholeness, the experience of which we won't understand until we get there.

MINOR ARCANA

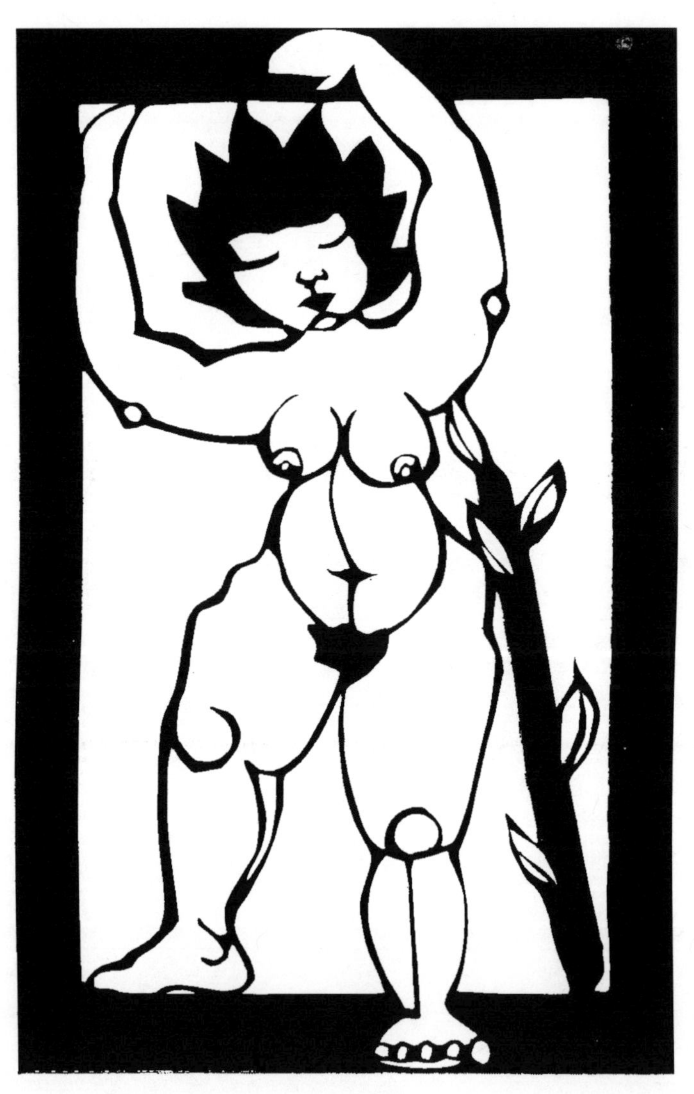

Ace of Wands

creativity, beginnings, invention, centre of fire

Arms above her head, hair tall, this dancer is sturdy but not on level ground. Her eyes are closed and her mouth is relaxed. Her wand leans on her thigh. She is ready for things, and they are just pouring in, calling for her to grab onto them. She is strong, and aware, and full of passion, but also open to change. She has faith that things will work out and is not afraid of what will happen next.

Aces open us up to the raw energy of a suit and its element—in this case fire, and its potential for enthusiasm, creative success, victory, ambition, exciting conflict. Sometimes people are scared of fire's symbolism, but if you pull this card, it's going to hit you whether you fear it or not. In fact, the card is suggesting that you open yourself up to it, because it is going to come rushing at you: the roar of a wild new relationship, an idea finally crackling into reality, your ardour for life revived.

When you get this card in a reading, it signals beginnings, fruition of creative potential, healing, opportunity. These things are surging in, homos, and it's up to you to be open and let them move you.

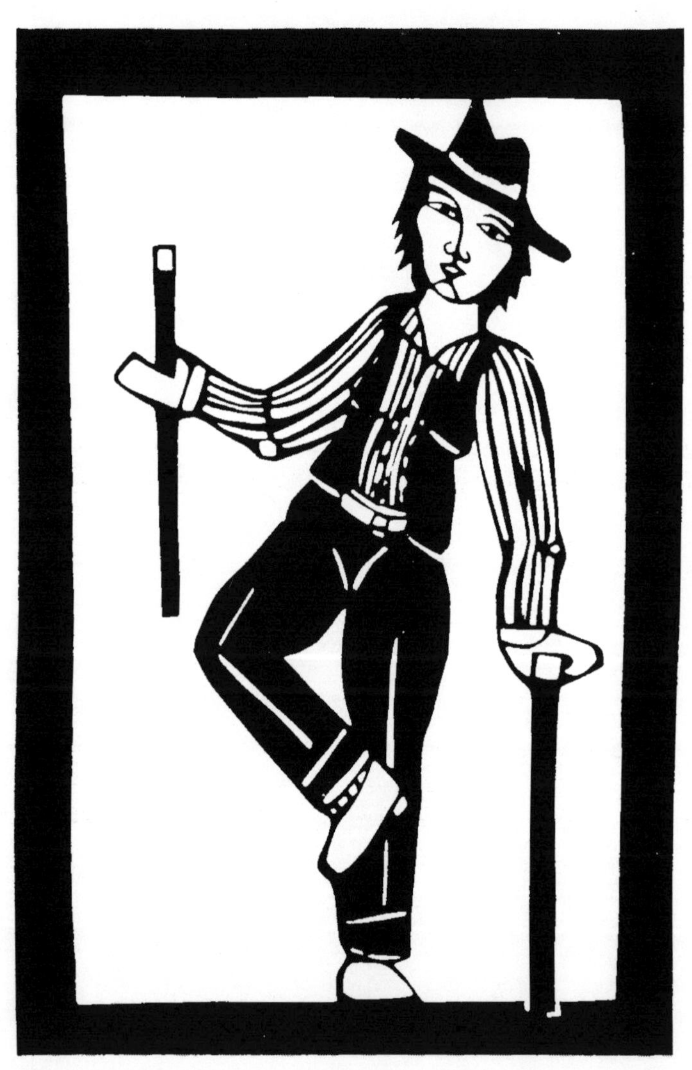

Two of Wands

success through practical skills, mastery

The performer on this card is alone, a wand in each hand. One is being used for balance: the balance between inner and outer worlds, and the balance within relationships.

This Two draws out your potential to develop inner focus leading to variable success—the variation of which lies in whether this process is effective and pleasant for you, or whether it is restrictive and isolating. Probably it is at times both.

So way to go! You may be a little lonely or lost, but you have some structure. What's off balance in your life? Are you willing or able to find stability from within your conflict-driven psyche?

In a reading, this card points to personal success, which often comes on the heels of a little soul-searching; or to a new relationship, which may be in conversation with that internal work, or for which the conditions were made by whatever accomplishments have come from your self-knowledge.

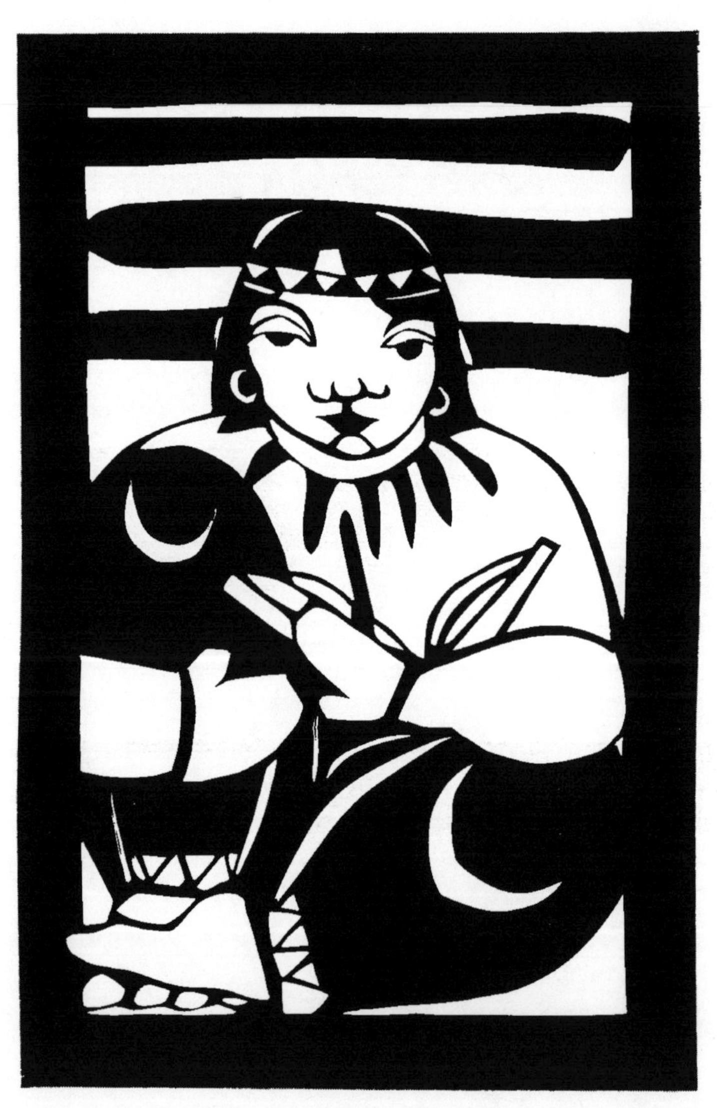

Three of Wands

solid, dependable, commerce and communication

Wearing a headband and earrings, this person has moons on their pants. They are seated. Three wands line up behind their head. The moons bring water imagery into this fire card, suggesting a depth of emotional experience, an ability to abandon ego for the sake of the larger picture.

The Three of Wands promises achievement, excitement, and success, coupled with the idea of community support and luck, and also with exploring the unknown in a broader way, leading to depth and awareness. You're dressed and ready to go, emotionally spirited, and studious to the point of getting there.

If you get this card in a reading, here you are: far-sighted, adventurous, and optimistic, you have solidly achieved something, probably with the support of others. Now you can push through until it's entirely complete, and recognize the new and lucky route you're on. Also, this could be a time to let go of lingering energy spent on dwelling in the past in order to clear the way for what you have lined up, for the extremes of what you thought was complete but is getting even bigger.

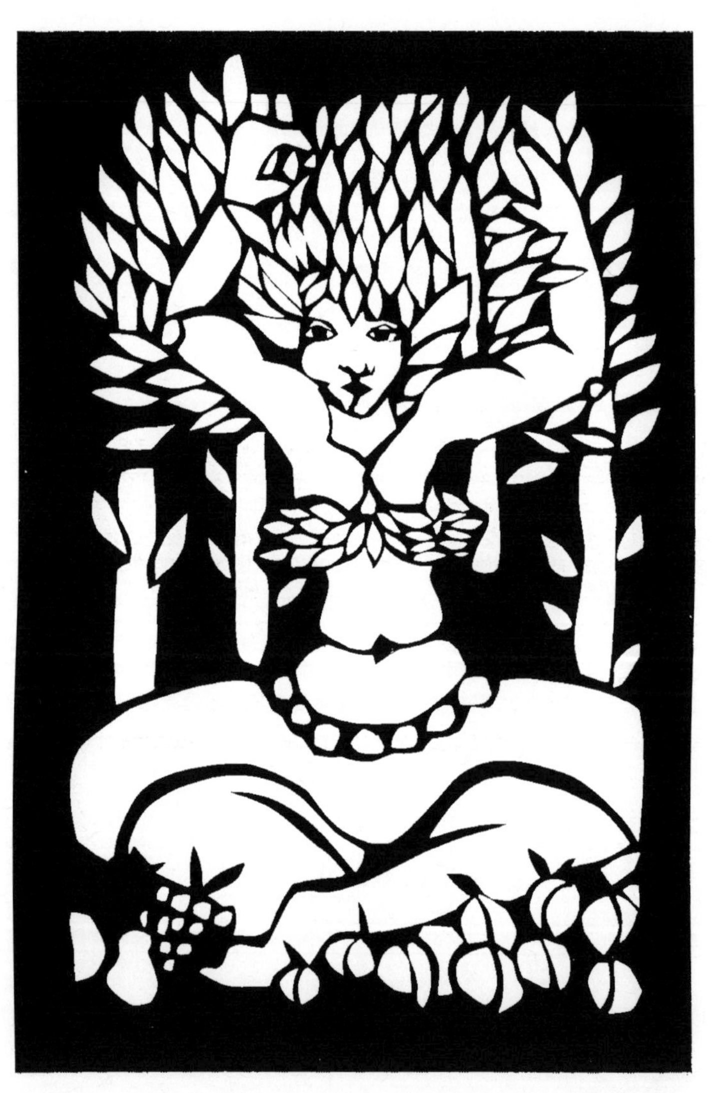

FOUR OF WANDS

bounty, security, attainment, and prosperity

Hello! Look who is growing an unstoppable halo of hair out of the leaves that also make up their bra. Their stomach is pleated with fullness and calm, their face determined and focused, but relaxed. They are seated, but their arms are in the air, brushing through their hair, ready for anything. Also look at all those fruits by their feet!

Fours are cards of structure, sometimes to the point of enclosure or captivity. Not for this guy. In its optimism, fire won't let itself be contained, and it instead takes the discipline of the number to grow until it bursts free before submitting to something it doesn't want to. Before a repressive situation has built up intolerably and has to explode to allow for growth, in the Four of Wands, your joy and enthusiasm draw you, celebrating, out of a defensive situation at an early stage. Your hair grows as one with the trees around you, and the fruits are at your feet, but you are not trapped.

This card in a reading predicts domestic harmony, creative discipline, romance, rewards for hard work, security, enjoying the moment—all qualities that develop from a happy union of will and spirit. Sit in that fruit or those woods. Comb that hair, but only as much as you want to. Sink into that love affair. Hold your hands up and run around outside of that structure, never letting it restrict you.

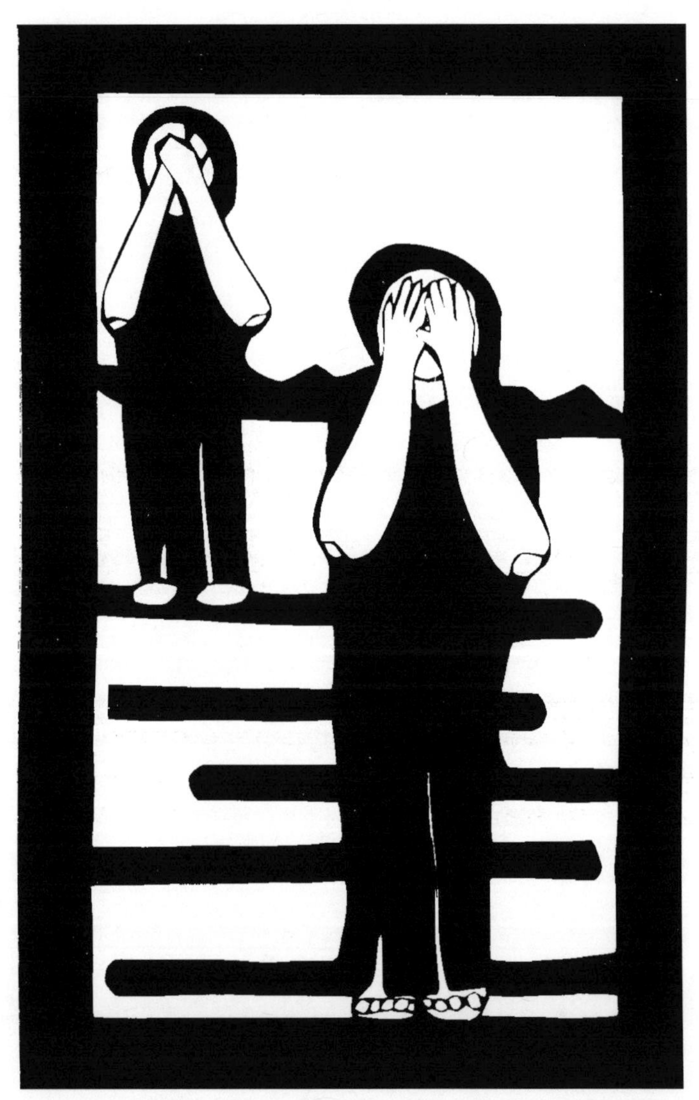

Five of Wands

strife, conflict, powerlessness, loss

The Five of Wands is still and remote. The characters' wands are placed on the ground in an orderly way; their faces are in their hands.

Fives are always about conflict but also communication, and fire, as we know, thrives on conflict. In this card, the latter may have gone too far, and you could be scared to face the damage. Something got razed, fell over, got shoved and jostled until it broke or burned to a crisp. But lots can grow after a forest fire, for example, and here you are, burned clean, ready to spring up through fresh soil.

It's possible that the people depicted here just need to uncover their eyes, face their shit, and get through it, which is ultimately the message of this card when it comes up in a reading. Sure, things are stressful and possibly competitive, but you have the strength to battle it out, start saving what you need instead of destroying it all in an instant, and move forward with zeal.

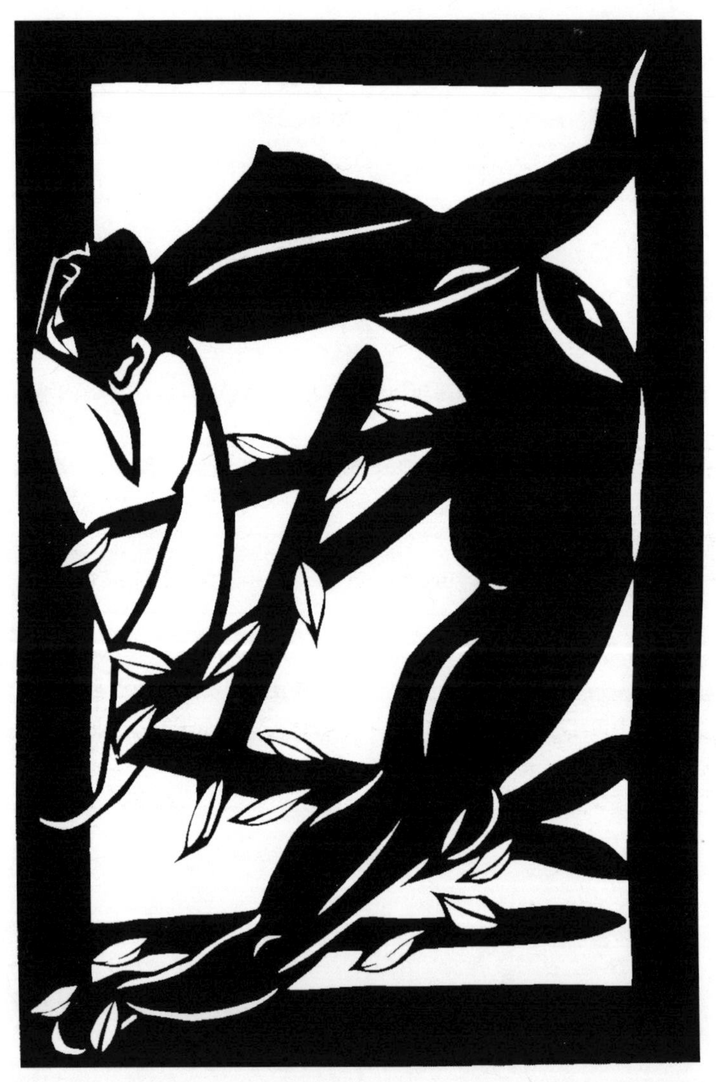

Six of Wands

expansiveness in spiritual or artistic matters

Bent backwards, this woman thrusts her pelvis up against one wall of the card, her hair falling back and tangling with the wands below her. She hasn't finished her project, but she's doing a good job of believing she will!

The enthusiasm of fire is evident in this card. Sometimes all you need is to believe you and your buddies are going to pull something off in order for it to happen. The obstacles, in your own head or en route to this triumphant moment, were tremendous, and you devised a way to remove them.

In a reading, this card reminds you that sometimes it's simply optimism—regarding collective or personal gifts, possibilities, and talents—that stirs up victory. Having won for today, you can use the afterglow to be graceful in your future losses and also to support others in their own feats. Sometimes somebody else's hair is going to be all tangled up in their project, and you're going to be watching them get an award for their work. And that's also pretty great.

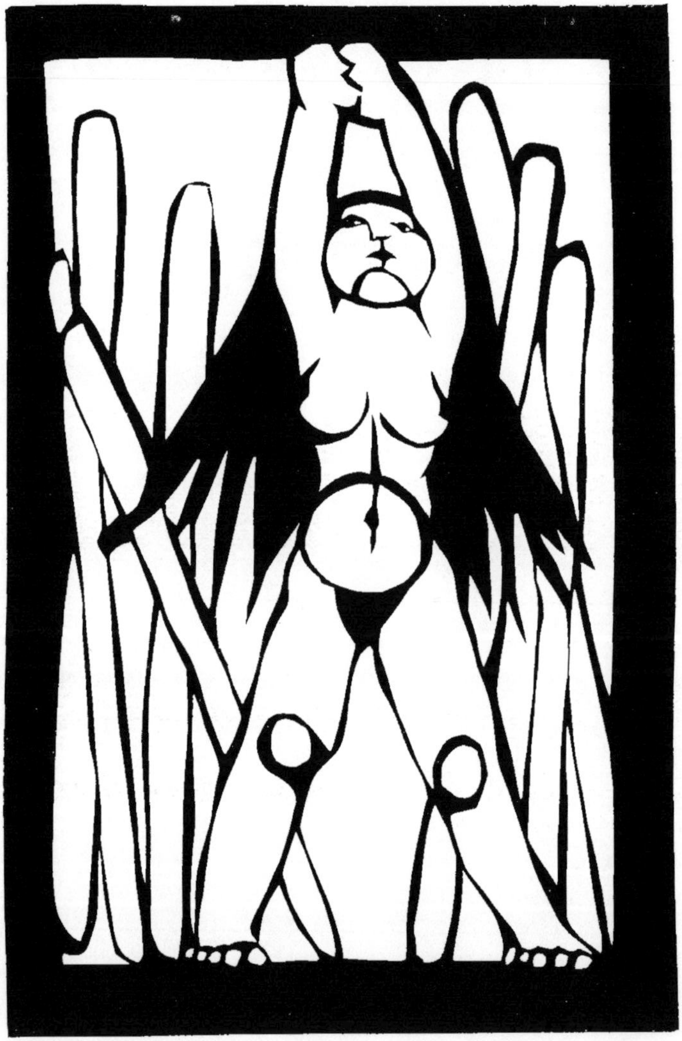

Seven of Wands

courage through unresolved difficulties

Despite being surrounded by conflict, or at least its aftermath or detritus, this person's fists are in the air, imagining winning. Wands recognize the transformative potential of confrontation—and in the Seven that quality is at its best. Their ruler, fire, likes to push its way through hard times.

The Seven of Wands suggests that you have an abundance of inner strength and determination, and you'll make it through and then move on to the next hurdle. But implicit in the whole suit is also a suggestion to rein in this kind of energy, occasionally, so that it doesn't build indefinitely. Conflict increasing forever can lead to imbalance, and if your neck is creaky with tension and your eyes won't close for hypervigilance, perhaps it's time to let someone else take on some of the fights and to rest before the next one.

This card in a reading allows you to imagine yourself forging ahead, in concert with your allies, out of a long-term oppressive situation; demanding what you need from someone in a position of authority; voicing what you need at all, to anyone. This is you making it clear, even if it's hard, and even if it means fighting quite a lot. This is the energy of being active against hardship, oppression, injustice, and of not losing your drive.

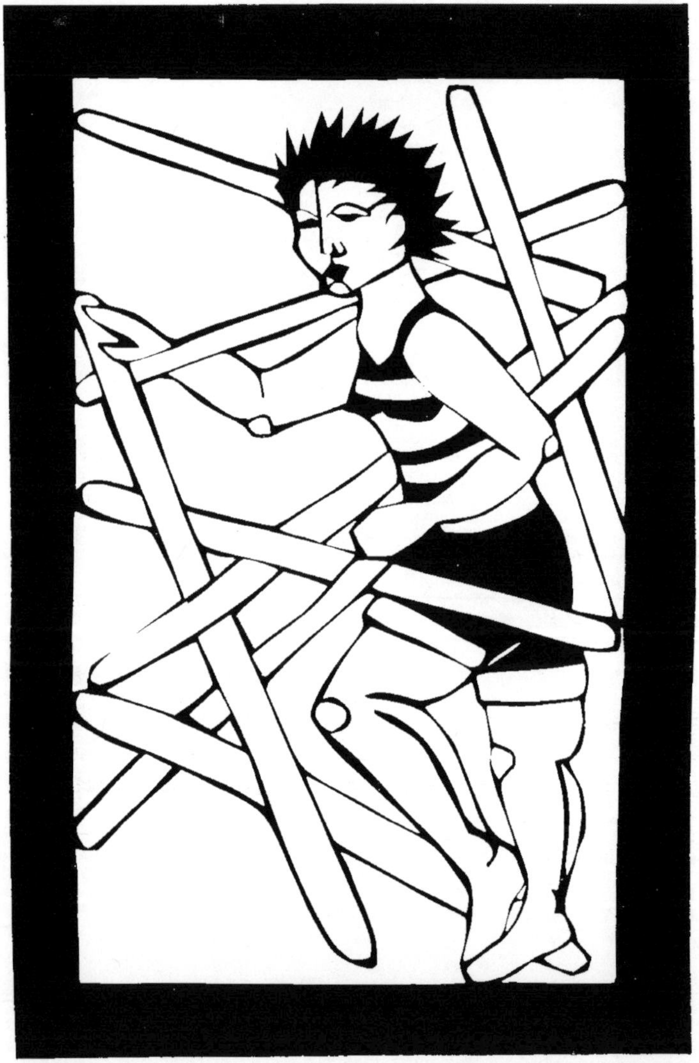

Eight of Wands

haste, mercurial motion, momentum, racing

Here's someone really tearing through obstacles, barefoot and sleeveless, ready to bruise up their legs with the effort. They're full of motion but also getting results—this card suggests some level of grounding of the wands' restless energy.

Because here you are, clattering through a sea of wands, when you could obviously go around it. While implicit in wands is the enjoyment of obstacles—daring yourself to release that album, face that conversation, bike through the winter—a necessary balance for that manner of approach to life is the peace, however brief, that follows on the heels of making it. So you grow more when you're pushed to, but you also have to have a second to notice that, and revel in it.

You're probably feeling restless still, but if you can just stop and admire your work, when you get this card, you'll realize you've made it. Try not to fight unnecessarily all the time, because you'll get exhausted, though some exhaustion is just great. You can feel the adrenaline rushing through you still, and it's glorious.

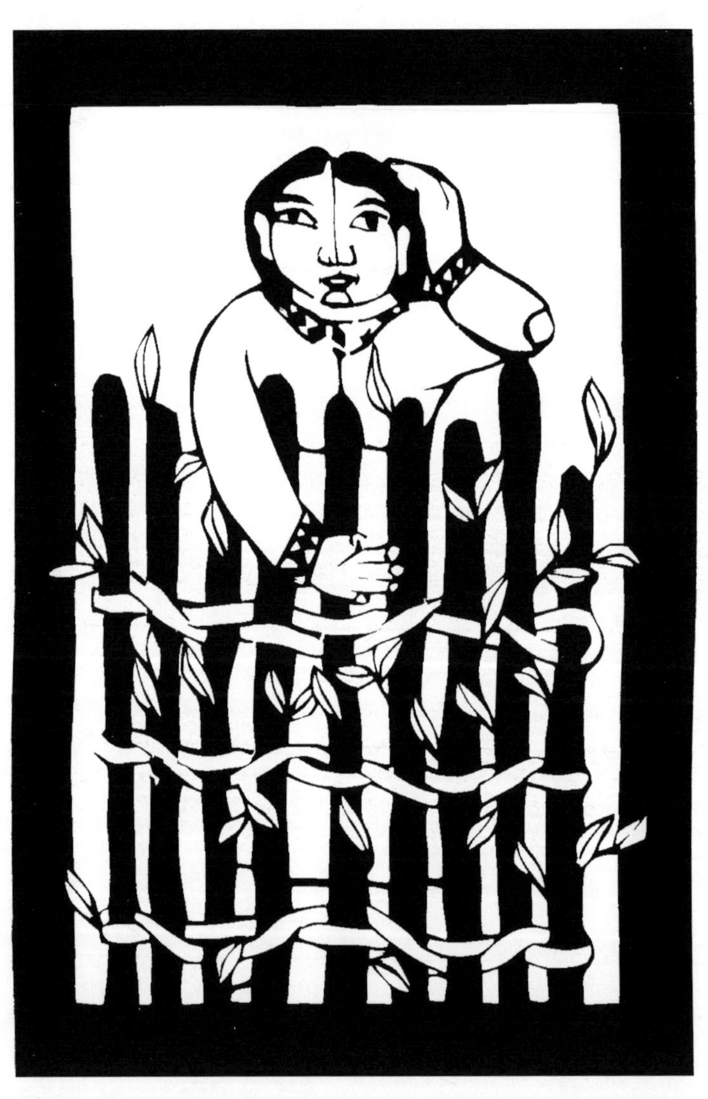

Nine of Wands

defence building, self-protection, reserve

Fenced in by wands, which are tightly woven together with vines, this person clutches the fence with one hand. Their clothing reaches up high on their neck and to their wrists, and their body is largely invisible behind the barrier. This is someone who knows how to protect themself, and how.

Sometimes you really need a fence; and the time and effort it has taken to weave those wands together is commendable. Sometimes things come flying from the air and that hand on your head will keep your skull from cracking; sometimes you need to keep a bat near the door; sometimes you need pepper spray in your purse.

But sometimes these defences are unnecessary. Sometimes you have built up strength and faith in your own fighting and protective abilities so much that you forget to or don't want to try another approach.

When you get this card in a reading, think about your defences: Are your strengths that you've built up in the spirit of conflict and self-protection useful for you right now? Or do you want to let someone through the fence for a visit? You're great and you have a lot of protective and productive skills, but some of them can be relinquished for moments, to relax, sink in, love, communicate, or collaborate.

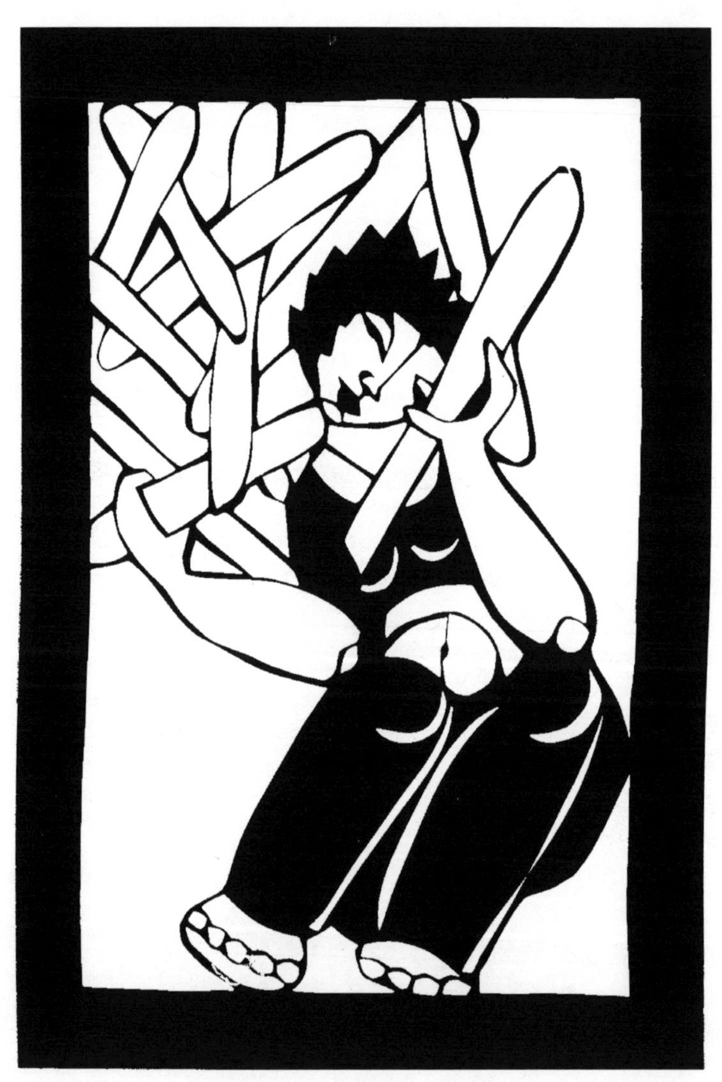

Ten of Wands

overwork, pressure, unnecessary troubles

What??!! This person is literally crumpled under a pile of wands! She is overworked, probably overwhelmed, and it's got her trapped underneath this heap. It's too much.

But tens are also cards of completion—this is the end of a cycle of labour or accumulation, and if you are able to delegate some of your responsibilities, lay down some of the less important tasks or even throw them all off (or let them be shoved out of your hands), you'll be prepared to start a new one.

If you get the Ten of Wands in a reading, you probably feel overburdened. This card suggests you think about how much you have taken on, how much of the emotional responsibility you are keeping to yourself, how much you can share with other people or whether you can ask them for help. Otherwise the cycle may end in a true burnout, where the wands' initiating energy self-destructs. Aim for generosity, discernment, and some level of thoughtfulness and calm so you can get shit done and also perceive its rewards.

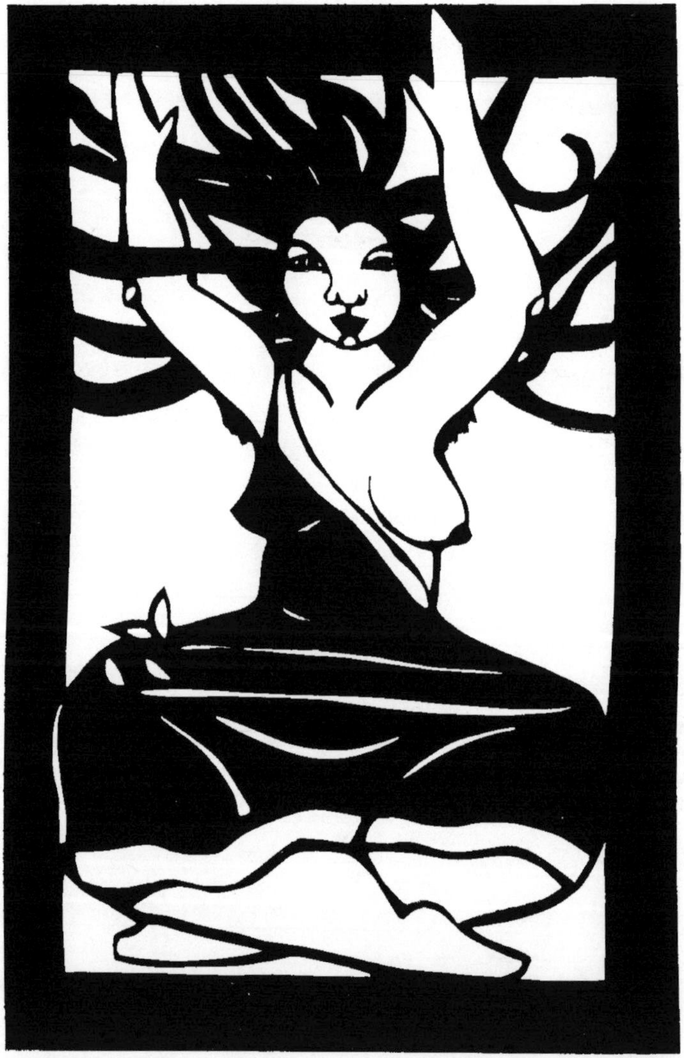

CHILD OF WANDS

reflective, faithful, spirit of fire

This figure's hair floats in an explosion around her head, right off the edge of the card. One pointy boob is caught in her clothing, and the other hangs to the side. She is cross-legged and some leaves have fallen on her. Her arms are in the air. She is wild! It's pretty fun being her!

Here is someone impatient but optimistic, and probably reckless. Who knows if she meant to have half her chest hanging out of her dress, but she doesn't care either way. She is cool.

If you get this card in a reading, please celebrate. It may indicate the need to study a particular subject more, but because of all the optimism and energy implicit in it, you'll be able to go for it. You might start new projects or relationships. It can also point to breakthroughs—the fire in this card combined with the curious nature of the Child can signal facing your fears to important ends. You've torn out of whatever limited, restricted region you were in before, and you are riding through an open area on a galloping animal.

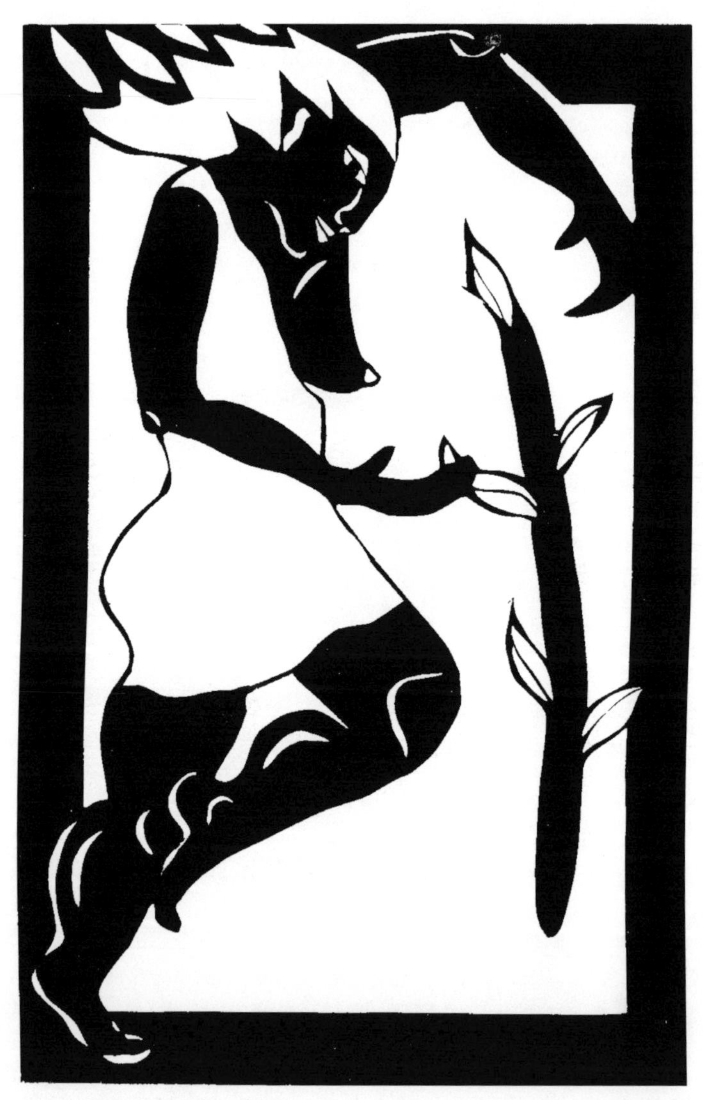

Wand Amazon

intense loyalty, soul of lasting relationships

Leaping forward toward her wand, head down, hair flying like fire, this Amazon is about to grab one of the leaves on her wand. All elements of the card suggest that she is enthusiastic about the symbol of fire before her—the problem with Amazons is that they sometimes lack strategy.

So like Sagittarius, the astrological sign typically associated with this card, while she may be focused and excited now, leaping into a conflict, project, or love affair, she may not be able to continue with it for that long.

Sometimes, however, that is just the kind of energy you need. In readings, this card can signify renewed ambition, focus, passion. Grab it while it's hot.

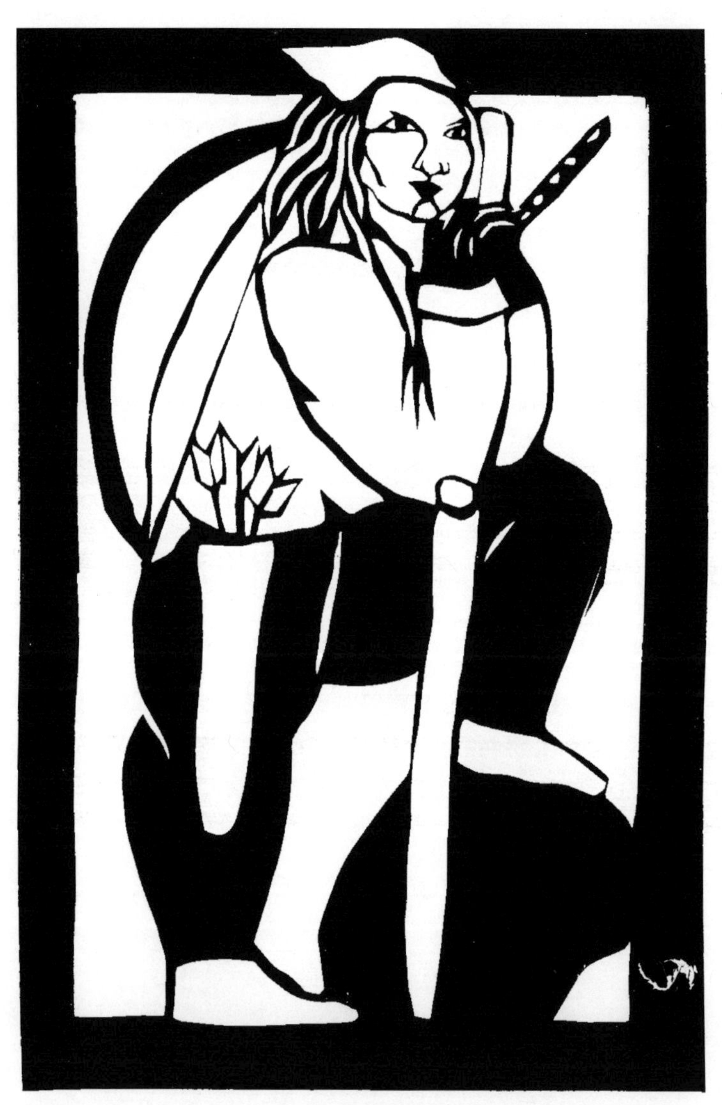

Daughter of Wands

honest, steady, hardworking

This lover/fighter has a quiver of arrows at their hip, a glint in their eye, a bow on their back, a bandana on their head, and their body is leaning forward into the future. Their mouth is set, generously but passionately fixated.

Here is a strong person, with a solid core that burns out their impact on the world. They can throw parties, be the best at school, perform all day. And furthermore, they inspire you to do those things too. They are also loyal to their friends and really good at taking care of their loved ones. This card is associated with the astrological sign Leo. Sound familiar?

The Daughter of Wands is enchanting; confident in their desirability and also full of love, they always seem to get what they need and want in exchange for what they give so freely to life. At the same time, they need some good—comfort, acclaim, joy—otherwise they risk becoming racked with bad feelings. They don't tolerate sheer hardship that well.

If you get this card in a reading, it foretells a time of magnetism, creation, and sexual fulfilment. This card wants you to open yourself up to these possibilities in a spirit of joy.

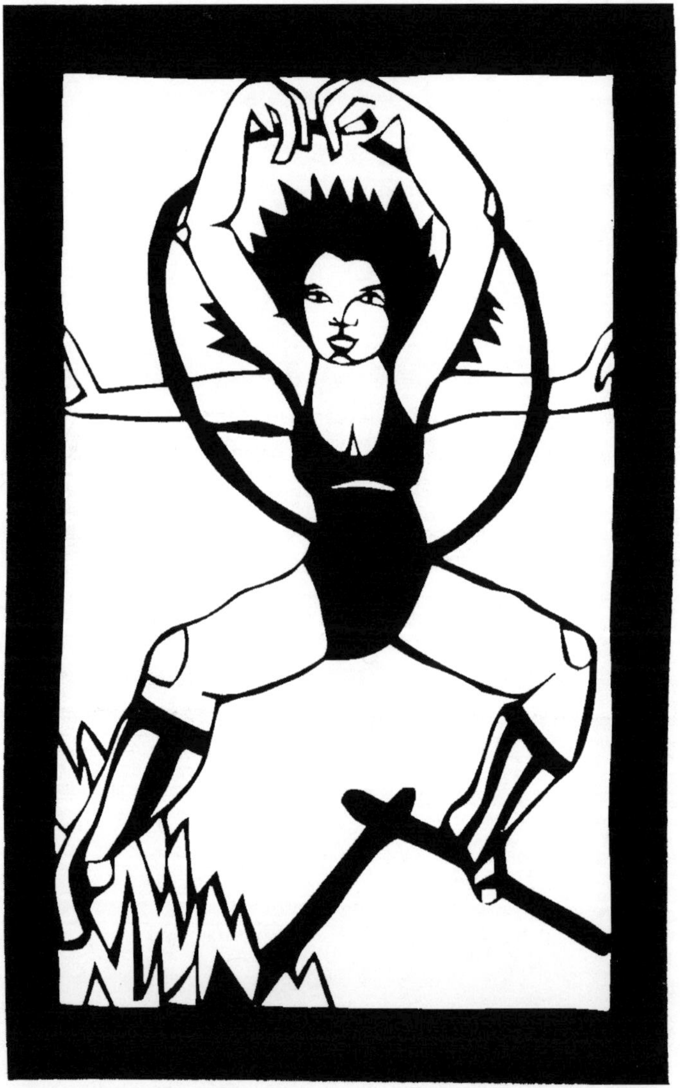

Wand Mother

spontaneous growth, heart of fire

Hula-hoops! Fire! Striped socks! That fierce look of concentration! This is the Aries of the deck, brimming with ambition, spontaneity, leadership, and creativity. Perhaps unlike many people's experiences with Aries-ruled people, this figure is also generous and perceptive about others' needs and experiences. And look, they have four arms, so they'll probably be rapidly helpful once they've perceived what you need. Plus, that bodysuit!

The Wand Mother has clearly developed self-mastery and is channelling inspiration. Someone with so much energy can get uncomfortable focusing on that one hula-hoop act all the time, though. At their most confident, the Wand Mother provides leadership and examples for others who wish to direct their energy. Their drawbacks can be rigidity and authoritarianism—also, the belief that if they can do it, everyone else can. But not everyone has four arms and knee socks.

If you get this card, and you have some creative goals, they are probably being realized or rewarded. You've put in time, and you've performed, and you've really outdone yourself. You might even be bored of your achievements. Hopefully you've gotten to a point where your life is still dynamic, and you've learned that mistakes are just disasters through which you learn more about your limitations, but also your possibilities.

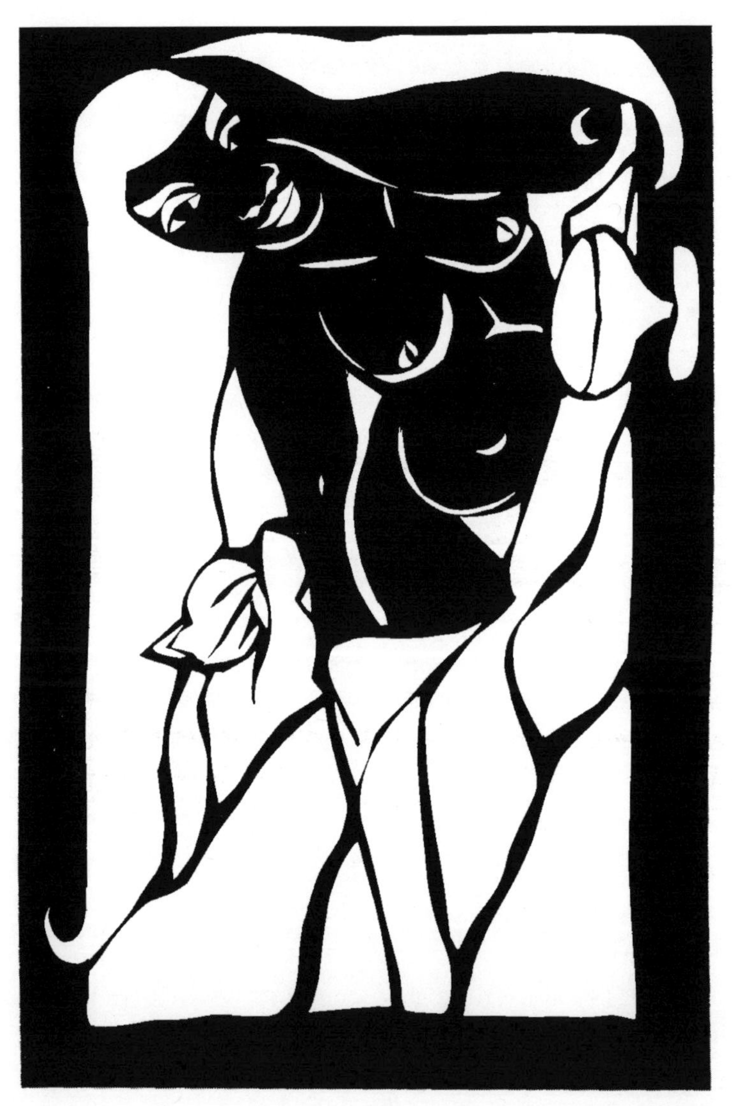

Ace of Cups

abundance, joy, fruitfulness, generosity

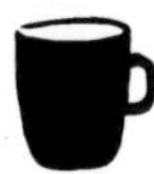

This dreamboat is partially wrapped in luxurious fabric, which is being made wetter and simultaneously more luxurious by a spontaneously pouring cup. Her hair falls down past the cat over her arm, which is propped against her ear, and which has a moon shape on the elbow. She is dreamy eyed, at ease, and in motion. Whaddalife.

This Ace's potentials are wrapped up in water symbolism. The card holds all the possibilities of cups in their seed state, so here you will find a small epitome of joy, or relationship, or spiritual connection. The strength and fluidity of this arguably strongest of the elements is visible in the design of this card.

When the Ace of Cups pours into your reading, it symbolizes a time of love and happiness, of receptive joy. Because as water is strong, it is also fluid, and so the quality of this joy is partly found in its receptiveness, its acceptance of life. Fall in; swim with the current; let the rain wash away your tears.

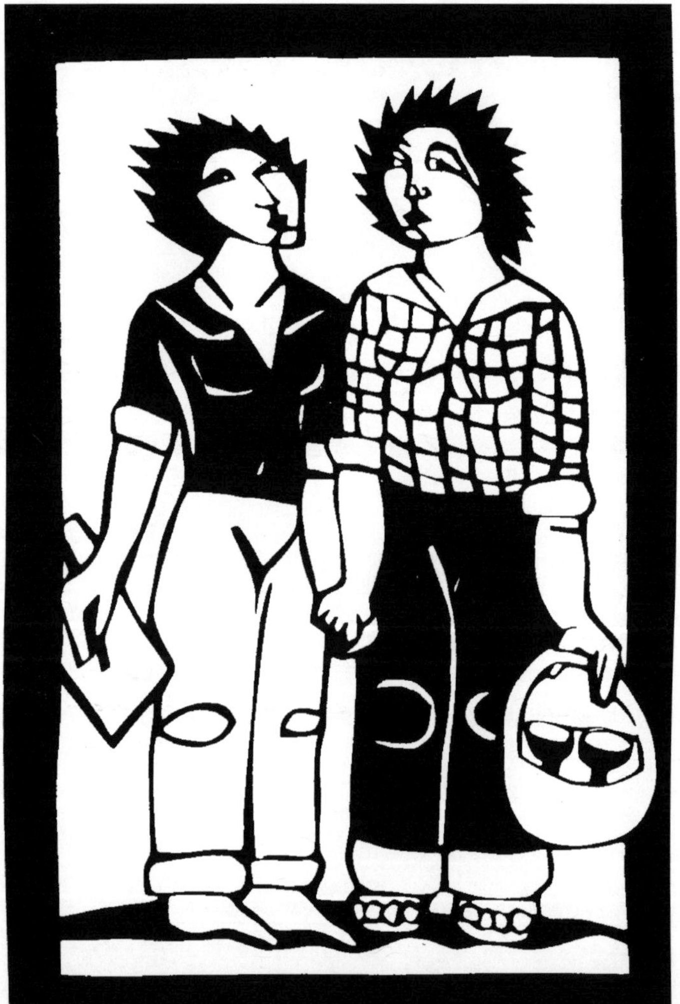

Two of Cups

love, enduring and harmonious relationships

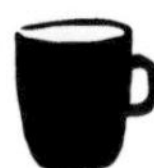

A Minor Arcana version of the Lovers, these homos are holding hands, unifying themselves in the beginning of a new relationship, reconnecting in a long-term partnership, or demonstrating the parts of self that can be connected when you allow for internal wholeness. Wine and pen and paper, plaid and plain shirts, shoes or bare feet, black pants or white.

This card signifies open and honest communication, shared energy, surprise gifts, or generally the power of two.

When you pull the Two in this suit of feelings and creativity, it suggests the beginning of a romance or other partnership. You've wrapped up your emotional life with rational thought, bound the two together, and created something meaningful—be it a picnic, a relationship, or a self.

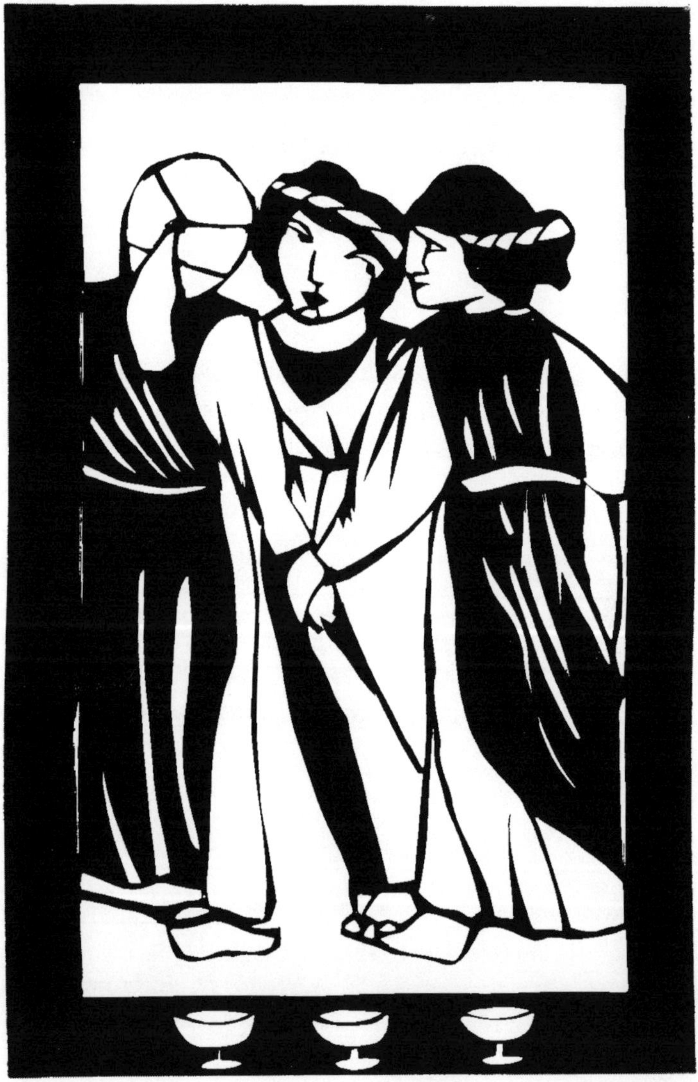

Three of Cups

goals attained through group achievements

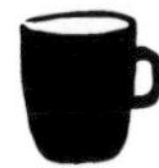

The friends on this card are turned inward, not into themselves individually but into the circle enclosed by their clasped hands. They are absorbed; they are enjoying their friendship and their mutual aid. They are satisfied as a group, and they are celebrating the completion of some goal or struggle.

The Three of Cups indicates fulfilment, related to the Empress' abundance. Support, inclusion, and care elevate the emotional lives of friends and lovers, and manifest in the birth of creative projects or in simple celebrations of friendship and beginnings.

In readings, this card points to the value of support among friends or an army of lovers—to the exponential gains that can emerge from shared experience.

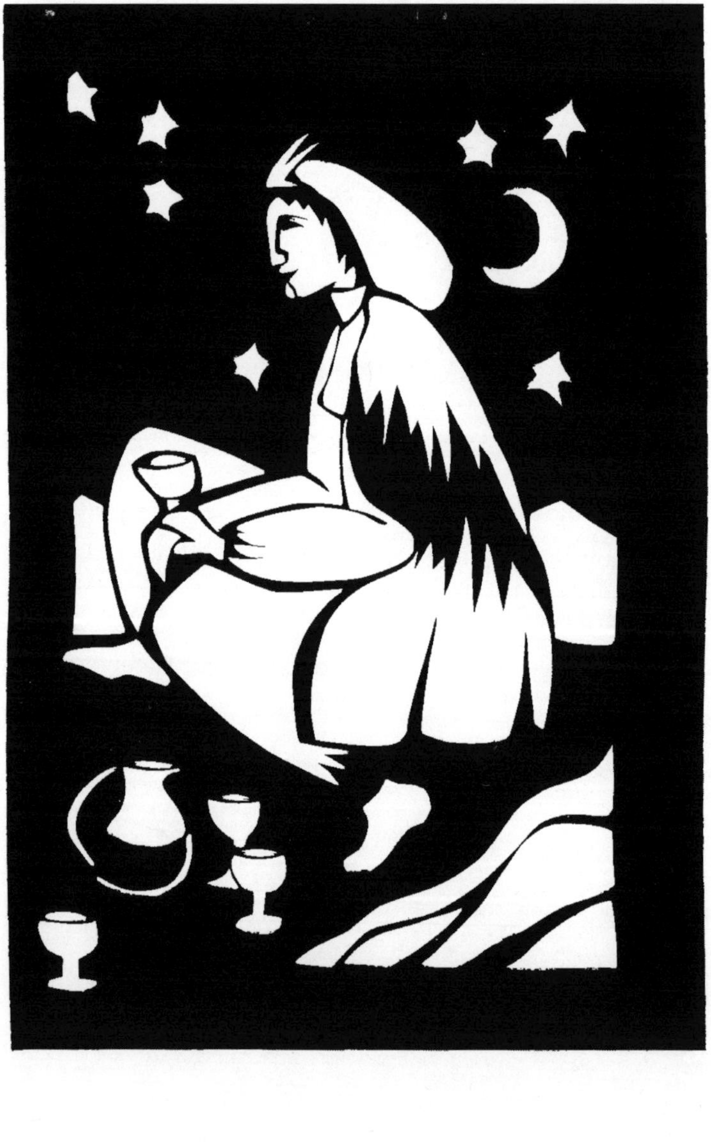

Four of Cups

reflection, questing, study

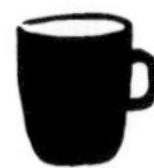

This dreamer sits by a river, drinking from a goblet, bangs blowing up under her hood, body draped in warm clothes. She is thoughtful; she is poised; she is sitting in the night. It's a beautiful scene but she's looking past it, or else is lost in self-reflection. She is also looking over the cup held in her hands, inscrutable.

The number of structure in the suit of creativity can mean an inability to feel good or see the value in your creations. This is when things go stale or sour. Either you can't see the worth of what you have, what you've built, what you're contributing to—or else you have grown out or are tired of it. Instead of trying to remain in a bad relationship, or endure shitty group dynamics for the security they offer, or stay living somewhere where you're unhappy, go deeper.

If you get this card in a reading, take hold of the fourth cup. You might be feeling unmotivated, but the cup you hold points to new opportunities, ones that revive your enthusiasm for life, if that's what you're going for. You may have experienced loss, but some possibility for success and happiness or simple contentment remains. Either you'll find exciting fresh things under damp overgrowth, and allow them to clamber up into the sunshine, or you'll realize it's all pretty rotten down there, and think more wholeheartedly about what you need, and where to find it.

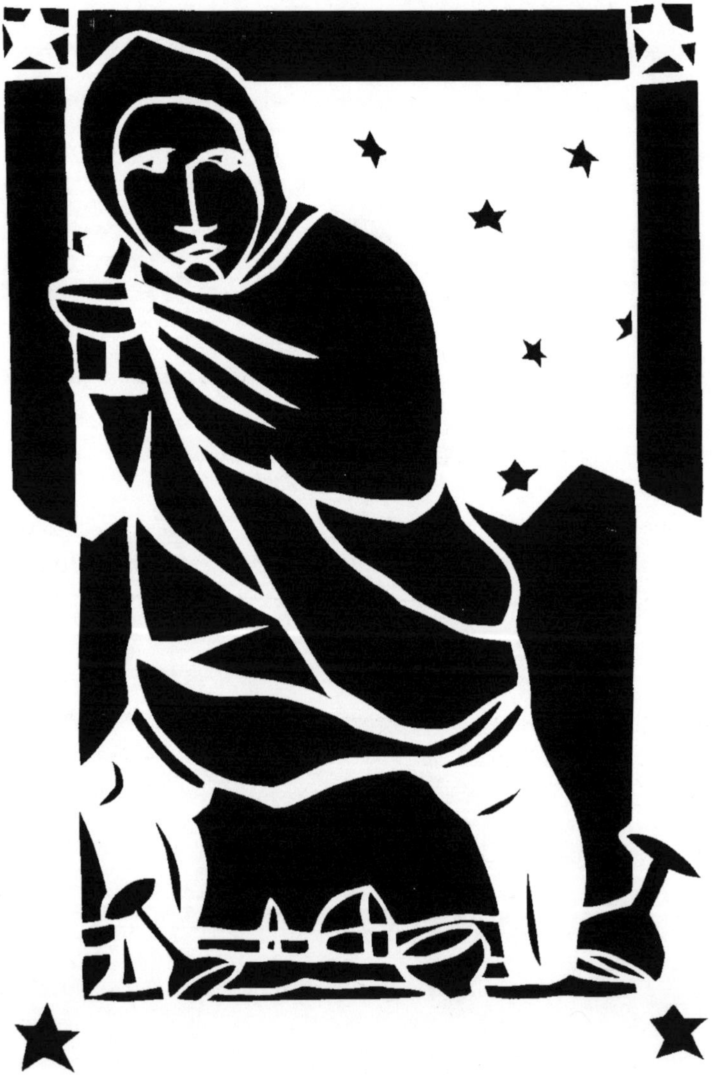

Five of Cups

retreat, disappointment, futility, neglect

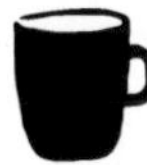

Look at that distracted face. The cloaked figure on the card, experiencing sadness over loss, carries a cup into the night, peering to the side away from it. Another four cups are spilled at their feet.

Moving through heartache can take a while. Possibly in a grieving garment, this person hasn't yet fully healed from their loss. They are distraught. But the Five of Cups suggests that they will heal, and once they do, they'll turn their eyes toward that final cup, watch the sunrise burn the night away, and see colour again after their period of separation, isolation, and mourning.

In a reading, this card reminds us that sometimes we have to let the upheaval run its course. While the card foretells sadness, it also positions itself in the aftermath of loss, marking the mourning process and symbolizing the possibility of growth or perspective through your remaining capabilities. These things that remain are in the cup that you still hold in your wrapped hands.

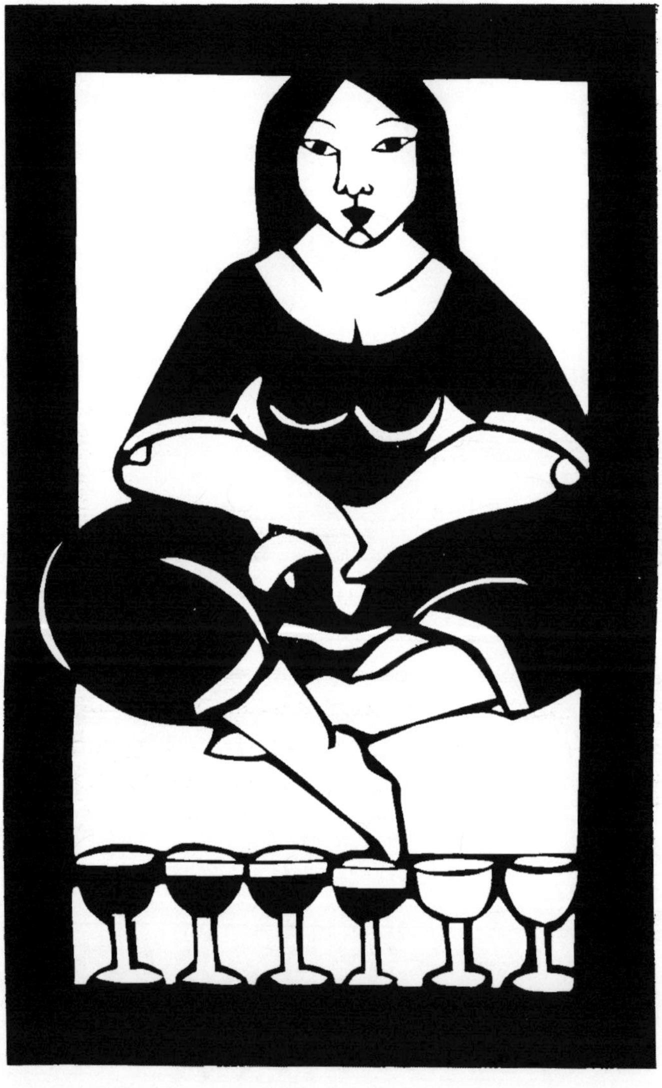

Six of Cups

strength, past insight helps striding forward

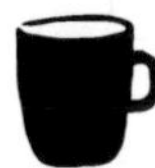

Wearing a boatneck shirt and cross-legged on the ground, the person on this card is seated, with six cups with sequential amounts of liquid in them lined up in front of her. Her face is solemn and contemplative, and whether the glasses are progressively more full or empty depends on her perspective.

This is a card of sweet memories but also of longing and nostalgia—sometimes unplaceable, and sometimes to the point of denial of the present. It reminds you that fixation on the past or indulgence in the familiar can allow you to avoid your problems.

Exchange is implicit in the sixes. You're a giver or a taker here, or both—of knowledge, wisdom, feelings. Hopefully you're able to draw on these gifts, without drowning in them, to fill up your present and future with similar gifts or extensions of those you have. If you stare too hard at that full cup, marker of past emotional satisfaction and security, you may not be able to focus on filling up those empty ones. At the same time, seeing the full ones is reassuring. A basis in comfort can give you the guts to move on.

The Six of Cups in a reading can encourage communication between long-term familiars, perhaps in a mentorship arrangement. Advice from a teacher, security in sharing a bed with an ex who has become a friend, or wisdom from a family member may come at this time. This card asks you to draw on the strength in your personal and collective histories, use your own memories and those of previous generations as guides, and heal through these low-key, domestic connections.

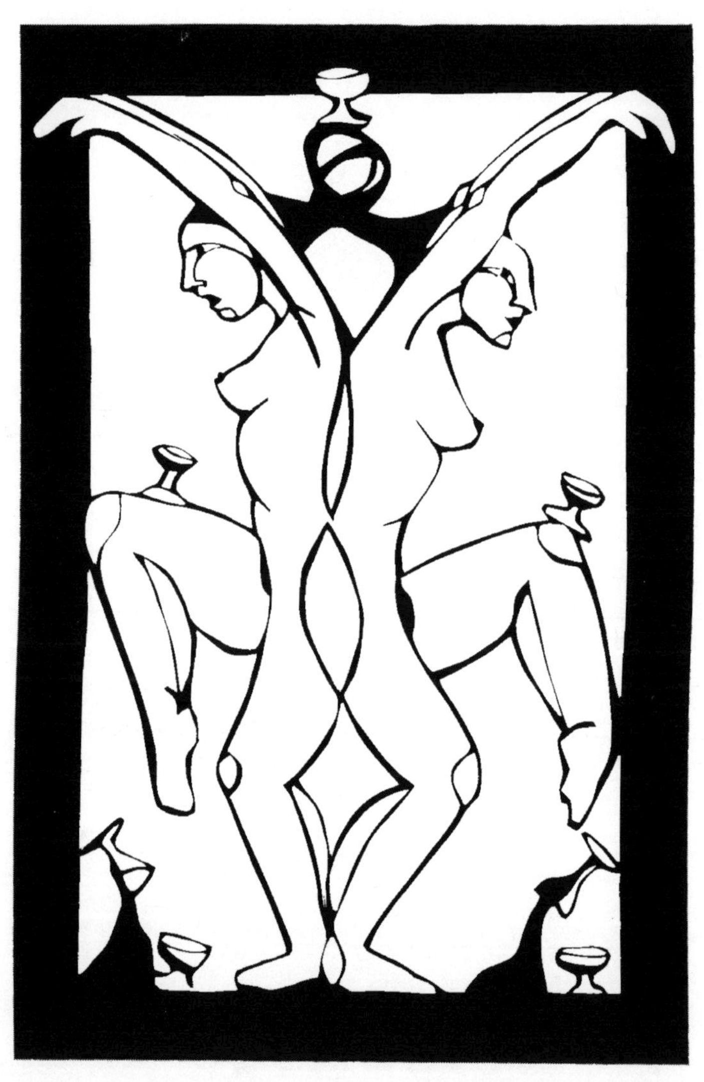

Seven of Cups

illusion, split choice, questionable success

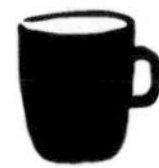

Two women stand back to back, balancing cups on their respective raised knees and in their combined curl of hair. Their faces have an air of concentration in profile, but each also appears to have kicked a cup over during their upward movement, spilling the contents.

There are too many things going on here. Why aren't they looking at each other? Their symmetry and the cup balanced on their spun hair are attractive elements in this particular rendition of the Seven of Cups, but what purpose are these things serving?

This is a daydream card. Sometimes we move in different directions internally, toward incompatible outcomes, as these women are doing. Cups on your knees, liquid spilled on the floor—your dreams form an intricate and intimate dance of valuable and exciting possibilities.

It can take time to make decisions. If you get this card in a reading, you may be working on turning your fantasies into reality, quelling your confusion, making a choice, or grounding some ideal. To invigorate this process, you could try directing your internal selves to be more in tandem, and putting the cups in some less reckless and precarious order.

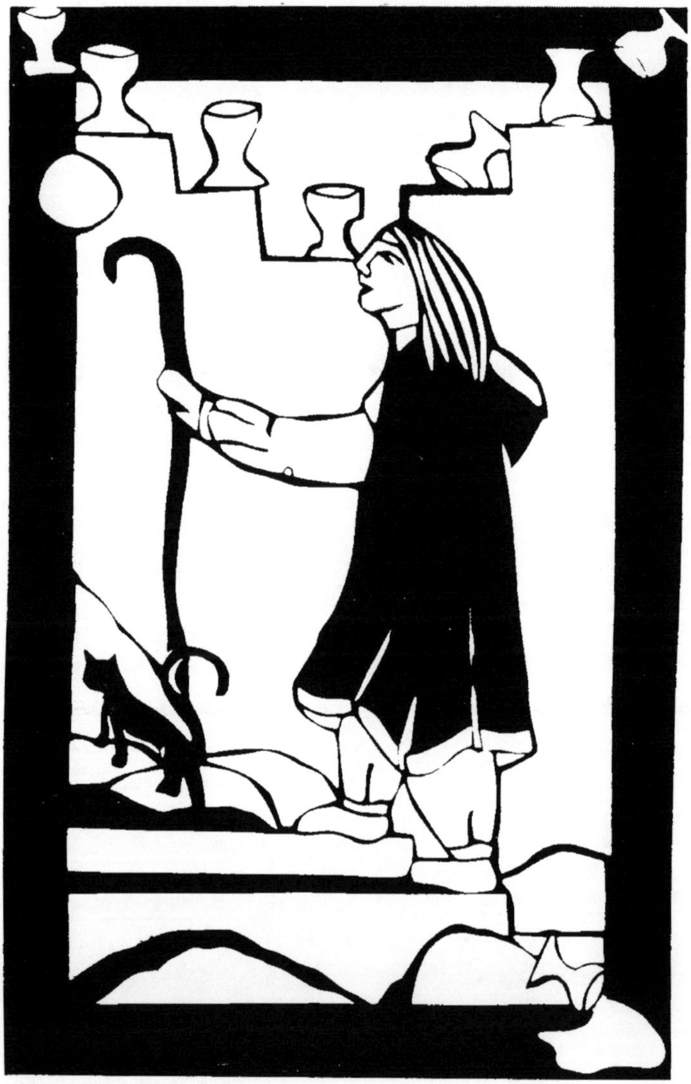

Eight of Cups

rejection, abandonment, moving away

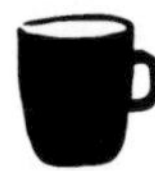

While not all the cups have fallen, this solo flyer is no longer looking at them. Instead, her gaze runs parallel to the wall on which they are placed and is directed up toward the moon. She has a companion, but it is a quiet, unobtrusive one—a cat. She also has a walking stick.

She has aid and companionship for her journey away from the situations or activities represented by the cups and toward some lunar knowledge. It is a solitary journey, one of retreat, sorrow, and ultimately, increased self-awareness.

When this card comes up in a reading, know that some level of withdrawal is emerging. Whether you have chosen to leave a situation before it has unquestionably ended, are staying attached to something that would be better left behind, or simply need a restorative retreat from the activity and duties of the world, this card heralds solitude. You may need to stop running away. Or you may need to move on.

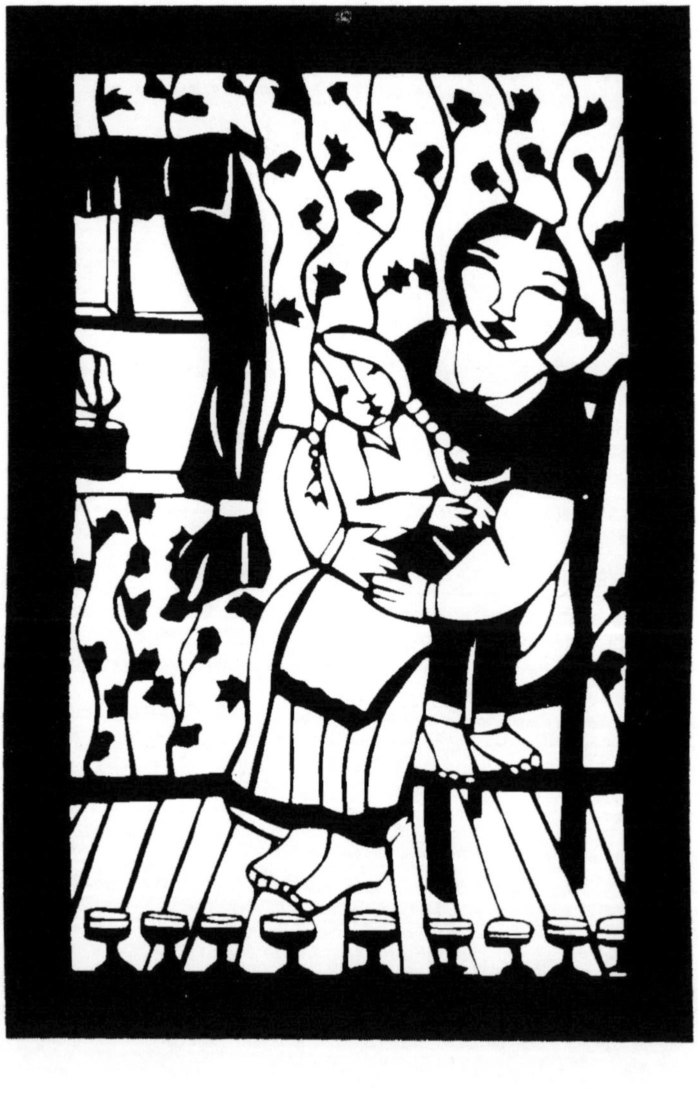

Nine of Cups

security, contentment, coming home

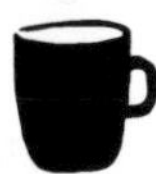

In a chair, a person in an apron sits with a smaller person on her lap. They are indoors, but curtains blow in the breeze, the wallpaper is attractive, and they are barefoot and calm. Nine cups are full at the bottom of the card.

This card represents domestic or general emotional contentment, perhaps even superficially or as brief respite from worry. These people might be having a nice moment after a stressful meal.

More substantially, when the Nine of Cups (one of the most clearly feel-good cards of the deck) turns up in a reading, it can point to winning, success, finally making it through, or reaping the rewards. Those orderly cups, that lively wallpaper, that loving embrace, and those matching braids might be your vision for your creative and emotional fulfilment, real and pulsing around you.

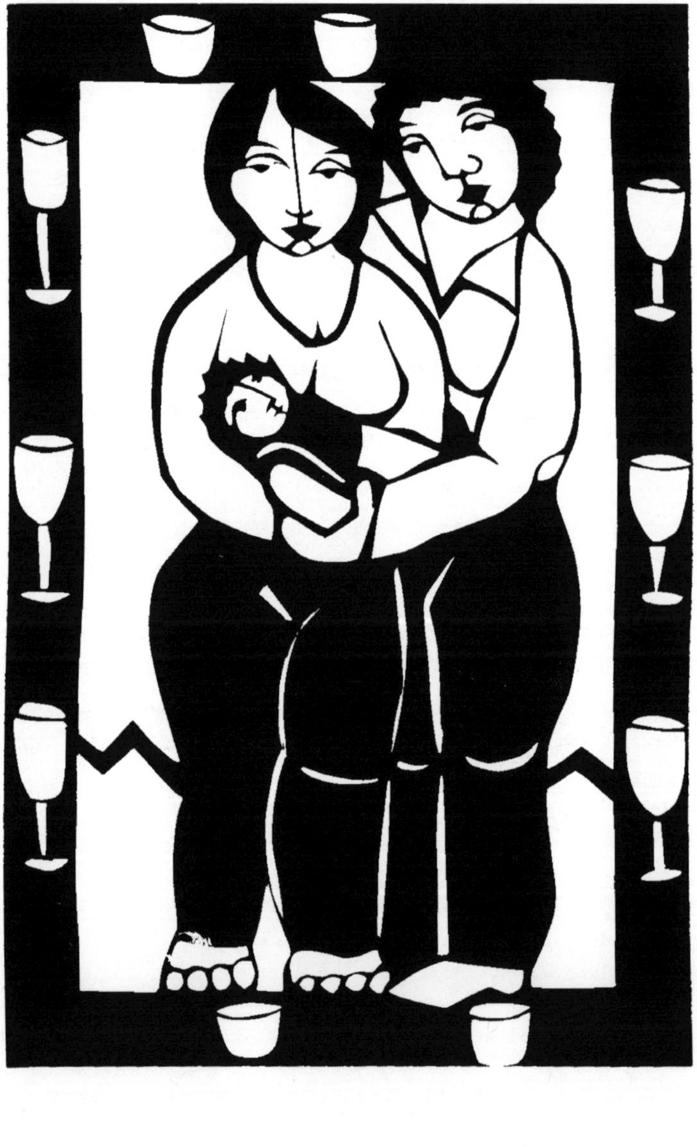

TEN OF CUPS

completion, nurturance, a sense of family

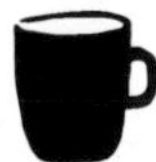

These gay parents are androgynous lookalikes, bumped up close to each other, gazing lovingly at their little child. They look calm, not that tired, and they're feeling good. Mountains loom unthreateningly behind them. This here is domestic fulfilment.

Tens, being at the end of a cycle, map out completion and therefore change—the kind that comes when something is intentionally finalized and stable enough to support whatever comes next.

Where this magical card emerges in a reading, you are happy with the relationships you have built, and they are harmonious. You are aware of your good fortune, and you understand that it took work to build. Your friendships, your community, and your other relationships are largely well founded and running smoothly, providing you with the nourishment you'll need for your next phase of life.

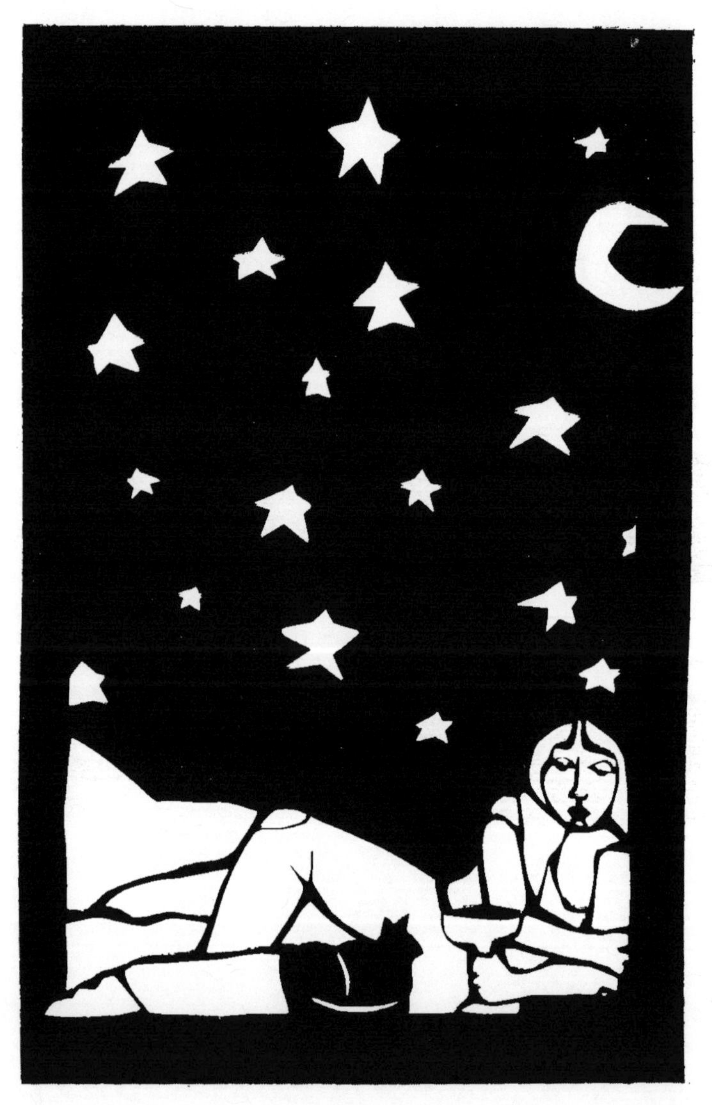

Child of Cups

discovery through reflection, clairvoyance

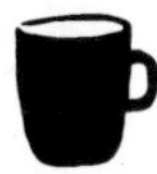

Leaning on their elbow in the outdoors, the Child of Cups has a glass of wine in hand; a cat is in the foreground. The majority of the frame is taken up by a clear night sky—giant stars and a crescent moon. They're lounging, face relaxed, eyes downturned, knee up, mountains behind them.

In its restful nightsky lounging, this card emphasizes freedom from outside distractions or worries. There's a small warning against jumping in too quickly, and it can veer toward sentimentality, but mostly it points to immersing yourself—into lovers, big feelings, all your dreams.

This is the baby of the suit of feelings and creativity—when you get this card in a reading, it's time to jump in. Open up—to an inpouring of psychic talents, the beginning of a love affair, imagining things for their own sake. Fall in, feel things, take risks.

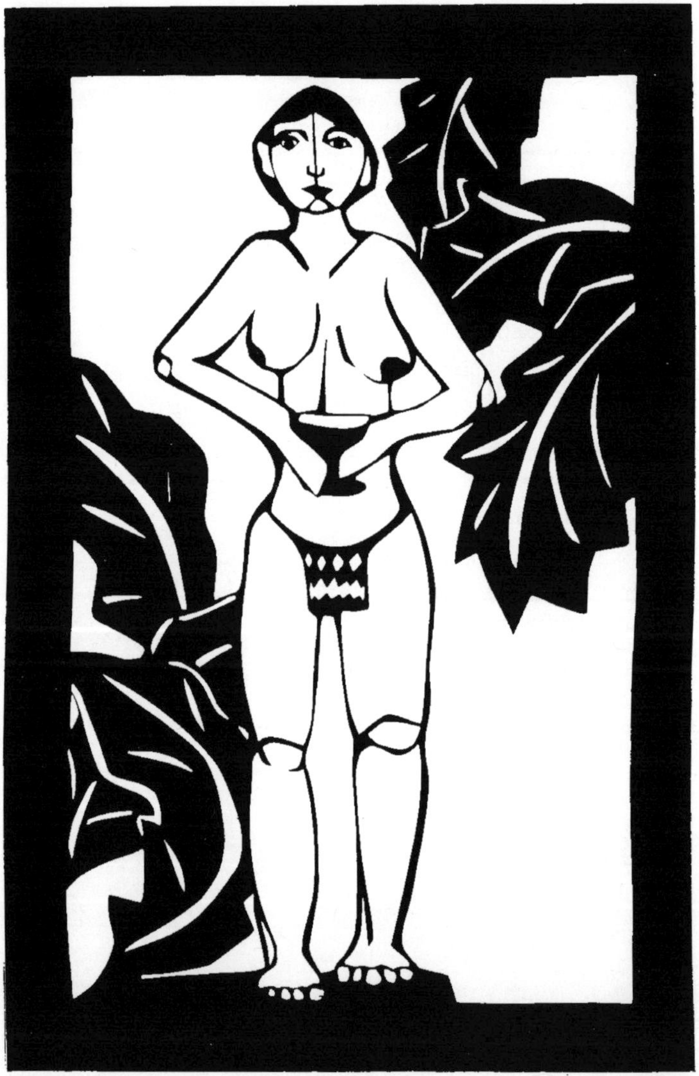

Cup Amazon

romance and pleasure searching, lover of life

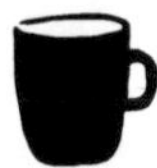

Staring blankly ahead, the Cup Amazon holds a cup at her navel, and lush foliage surrounds her standing body. She is naked except for a little flap of fabric or a codpiece at her crotch. It may not be a blank stare—it could be a dreamer's gaze. It could also be an internal gaze. Like the Pisces of the zodiac, with which this mutable feelings imagery is affiliated, this card allows the restless energy of the Amazon to be directed toward an exploration of the inner world.

With the bold but unfocused Amazon in the suit of imagination, creativity, and emotion, you can get lost in fantasy. Or you may pursue your dreams with a reckless admirable passion. Or you could be shallow—so while you might be well dressed or the life of the party, you may also be lacking profundity. In the latter case, you may be simply driven by attempts to escape the abundance of pain in the world, like a Pisces, and not by an overarching shallowness.

This card asks you to be reckless if you've been reining things in too much: Take off your shorts! Run through the foliage! Or to rein it in if you've been indulgent or fantasy driven to the point of your own destruction or dissolution: Hold your horses! Make sure that codpiece is on tight and externalize the ideas you've been too shy to explore! Drink less, work more!

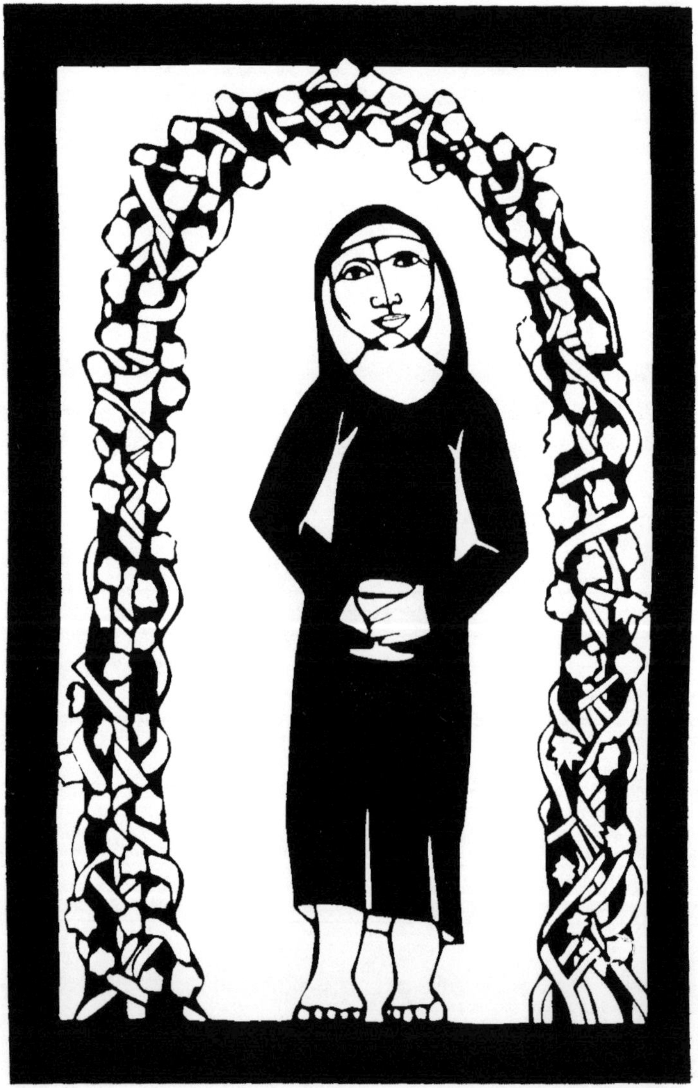

Daughter of Cups

generous, capable, calm, psychically talented

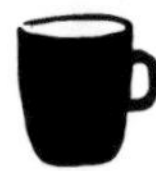

Long-sleeved, face forward, this figure looks out from their bower of flowers almost questioningly, but with evident clear-eyed compassion. They hold a single cup. Like the astrological Scorpio, with whom this card is associated, the Daughter of Cups represents a profound and focused collaboration of consciousness and feeling.

This person is harnessing their imagination and emotional power and directing it into artistic pursuits or social justice work. Others may find them restrained, protected in their bower, but also soothing if withdrawn, helpful if personally closed. This person will wrap you in their sweater, lend you the best book, and offer you tea or something else warm and necessary.

If you get this card in a reading, you are drawing on the ability or influence to do the same: to act on a foundation of love as well as a certain and focused understanding of global and personal circumstances, and to use these qualities to create useful and meaningful works.

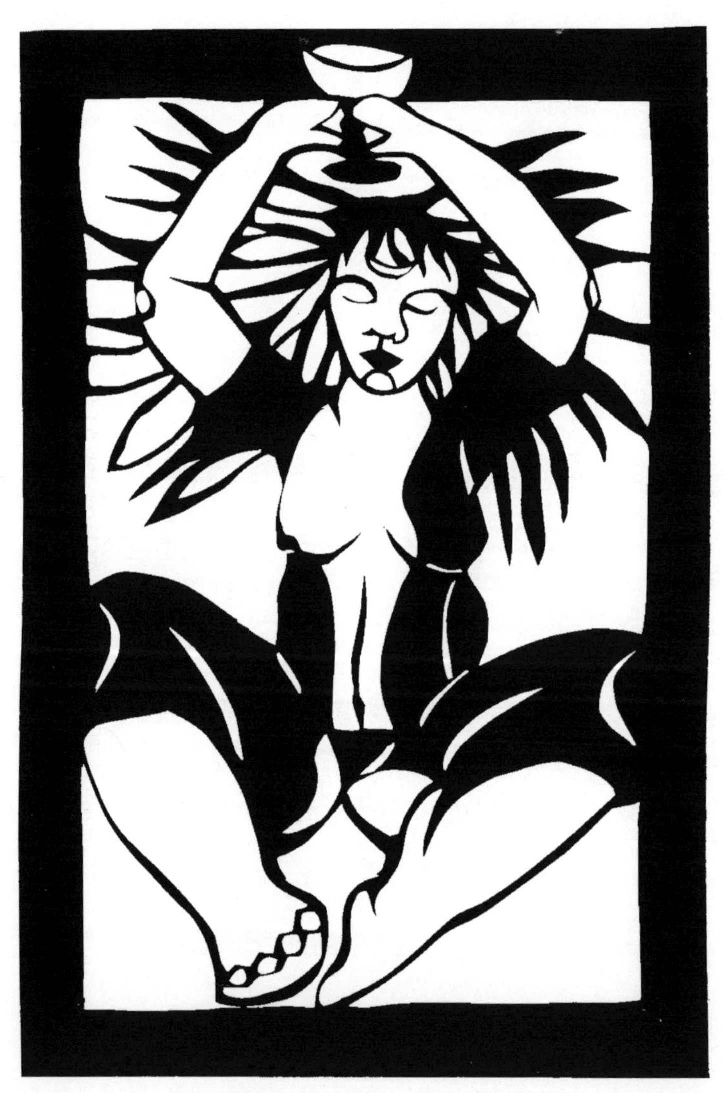

Cup Mother

devoted, sensual, heart of feeling and vision

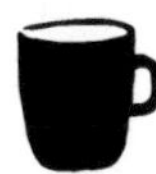

Her hair energetically flying out in every direction, this Mother sits calmly, eyes closed, with a cup balanced on her head. The containment of this feelings card is reminiscent of the zodiac's Cancer, traditionally associated with the Cup Mother, and with parenting, nurturing, and protection.

Here is someone who has taken the emotional or creative nature of the cups and given it shape and substance. The Cup Mother is wise and also responsible. Her powerful intuitive abilities are both helpful and difficult, because she can be full of passion but careful about revealing vulnerability. At her most self-protective, she is cut off from her emotions, or potentially deceitful. But ideally she acts as a mentor, an established artist, a conscious contributor to society, or a teacher.

If you get this card in a reading, it bodes well for mastery of your creative impulses, calm in a crisis, and sharing your hard-won wisdom. Here you are, hair exploding into a starburst at your will, sporting a specially designed outfit, giving other people ideas about their own potential for artistry.

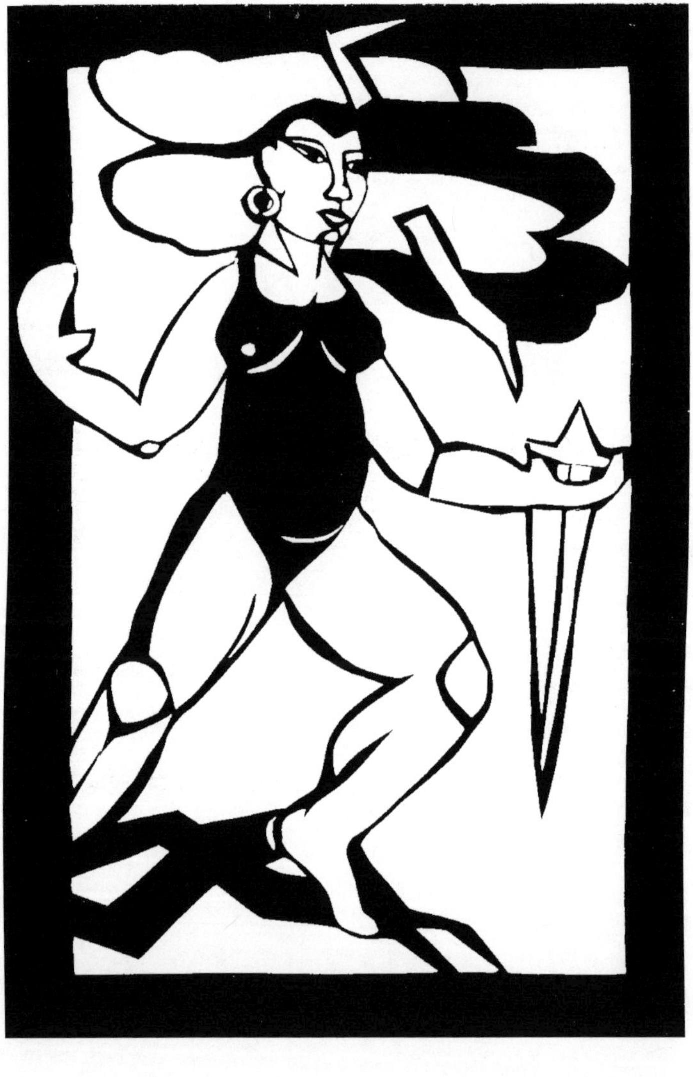

Ace of Swords

electric, strong action in love and hate

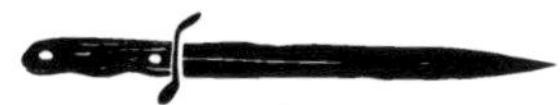

Above this go-getter, a lightning bolt pierces boldly through layers of cloud, representing sharp intelligence in the face of bleak or muddied situations. She herself holds a sword, symbol of mental clarity but also the pain inherent in pure rationality. She holds the potential to flip the earth-aiming sword around and engage in conflict. She is ready. She is wearing only a leotard or bathing suit—beyond her sword, she has nothing but her body and brain with which to defend herself.

Okay, just say it. After you've clearly figured out what it is. That lightning piercing the cloud, that lunge, that focused gaze: that's you speaking your deepest truths, which have been shot through the ringer of emotion, to temper them, but still remain clear. Look at the power in that stance!

If you get this card in a reading, it's showing you the possibility of sorting through the chaos of a pool of feelings but not rejecting it entirely, and also of the probability of powerful emotional communication. You figured out what you needed to say, you said it, and now you're dealing with the charged responses. Don't hold that sword up too high. But keep a little energy in those legs and that sharp jawline. You're standing up for yourself, negotiating some reasonable, workable plans, but it's going to take energy. An impersonal force is backing your brain and is ready to cut through and succeed for you.

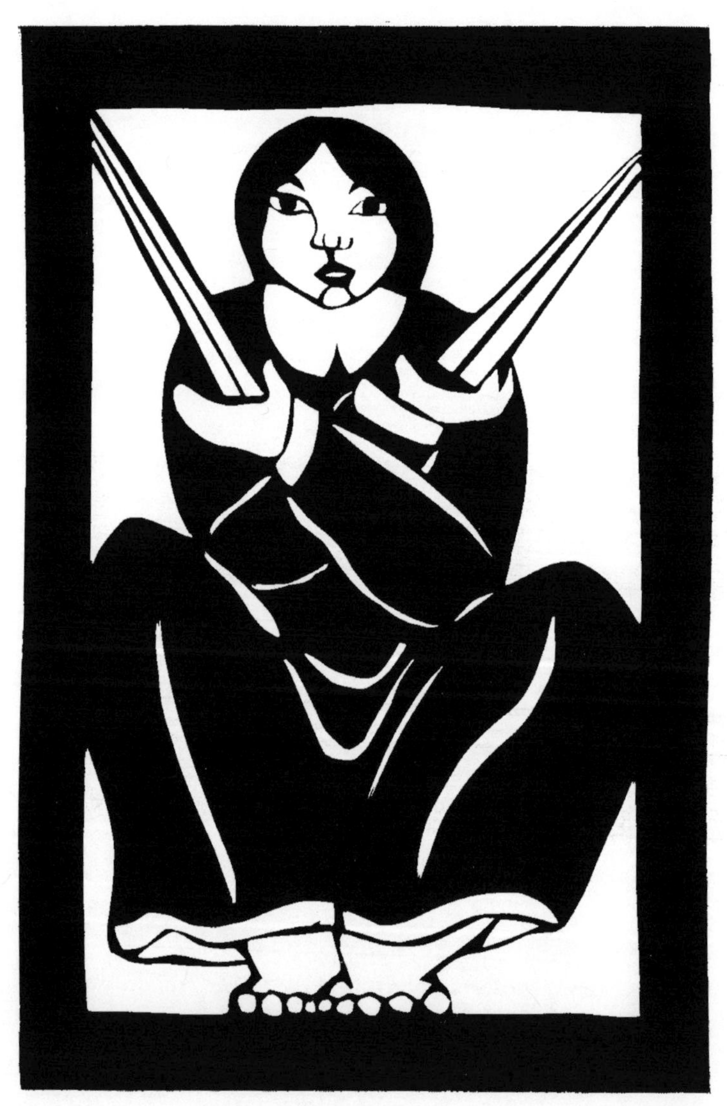

Two of Swords

truce, surrender under force, self-protection

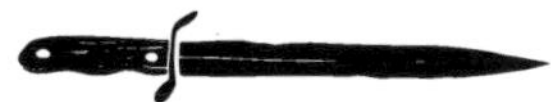

Crouched, arms crossed over her chest, this person holds upward-pointing swords. Her hair is parted and falls over the sides of her face; her eyes are cautious and her mouth slightly troubled. Her bare feet are together in front of her.

You might be a bit shut down but at least you're fair. On the one hand this card points to withdrawal from the world: you're taking some time for clear-eyed introspection and maybe retreat from conflict. That's okay, but it warns against going so far that you close your eyes and shut off regular communication to the point of not being able to access support later, when you need it again.

This card in a reading signifies compromise, diplomacy, and the ability to see both sides of an issue and come to an agreement, as long as you are clear on both parties' intentions. It also marks the balance between shutting down enough to converse calmly and rationally and keeping yourself open enough to maintain the emotional weight and depth behind your interactions. Out of kindness toward yourself, don't cut yourself off—it can be lonely.

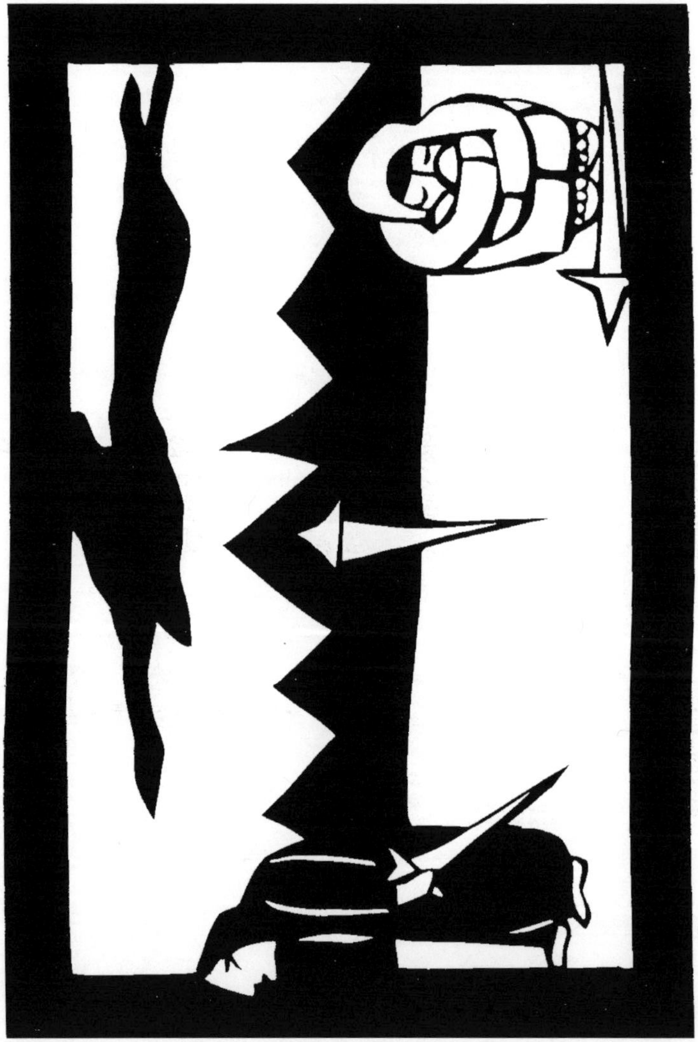

Three of Swords

grief, loss of loved one, melancholia

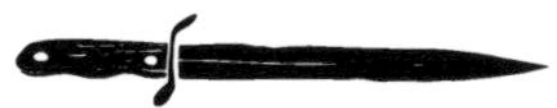

The image in this deck is less symmetrical than the giant pierced heart that many of us are used to, but it is similarly anguished. One figure, on the far left of the card, slumps and drags their sword behind them, appearing to lack the energy to stand upright or lift their weapon. The other, removed from the first by the horizontal length of the card, is curled up, arms wrapped around their knees, hooded, their sword at their feet.

This is a card at the intersection of communication and feelings—that broken and inconjunct position of irreconcilability or misunderstanding. If you weren't expecting that rational slice through your cushion of security—the logistics of long distance, the legal interference with how you make money—it could be painful. It is heartbreak, loss, sorrow, with the caveat that you can internalize and transform your pain into acceptance through love.

If you pull this card in a reading, it could be a hard time. You might do well by preparing for consequences after you've made a choice or remembering what you've learned from past challenges. The Three of Swords' transformative possibilities, premised on love, may eventually lead to necessary increased understanding and growth.

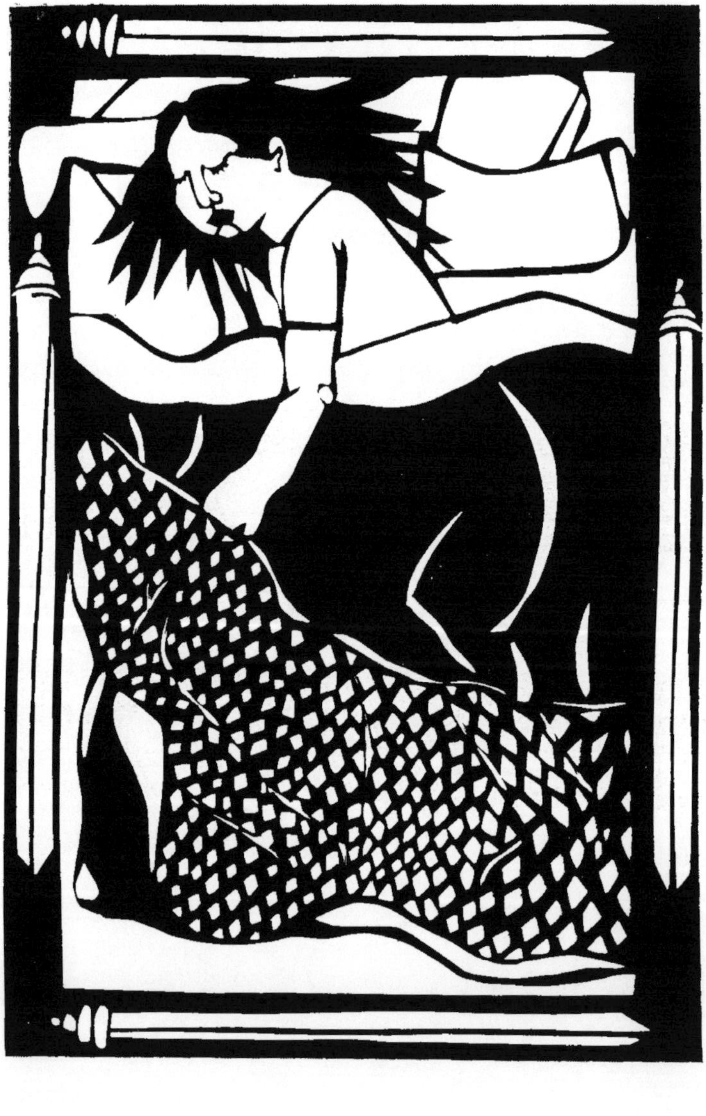

Four of Swords

stillness, rest, building of strength

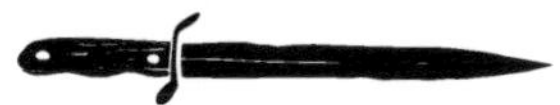

Her bed framed by swords, someone is napping, hair splayed on the pillow, hand clutching the top sheet. She is simultaneously enclosed and at rest, which is quite directly the intention behind this card—the structured implementation of relaxation and withdrawal.

Here we have boundaries, retreat, and respite from anxiety; shutting down and keeping walls up that block everyone out; and the balance of the two for your own wellbeing.

Depending on where it comes up in a reading as well as your usual level of assertiveness, this card could suggest unnecessary avoidance or much-needed withdrawal. Whether life is too overwhelming for you to drag yourself through it or whether you've been immersed in the public for so long you just need a break, you may need some rest in order to muster energy for whatever is next.

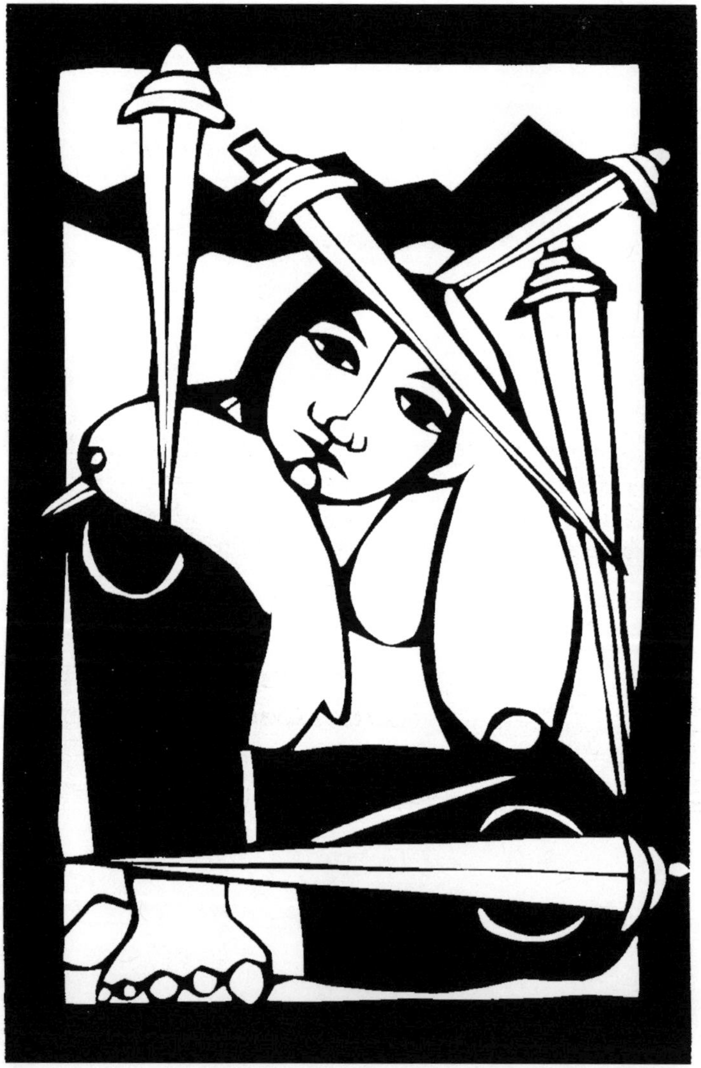

Five of Swords

pressure, mental chaos, internal struggling

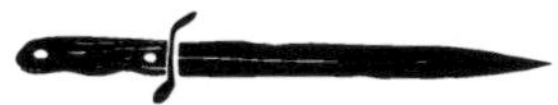

A single figure is boxed in by the edges of the card, swords surrounding her, including one across her forehead. She is folded in on herself with exhausted eyes. Loss, or a battle with any outcome, is exhausting.

The conflicted five in the mental suit of swords points to a sense of inadequacy, to defeat. Usually its focus is on the moment of defeat (less commonly, on the simultaneous moment of victory) or the period of despair that follows it.

In a reading, this card can indicate enemies—either broadly in a strenuous battle, or personally as an external figure or an internal voice of defeat. Productively, it can urge you to digest your hardship, healing in the time that you need to do so and moving in for another fight. With the freedom of one whose life has been dismantled, you are aiming for a win but recognizing the possibility of loss.

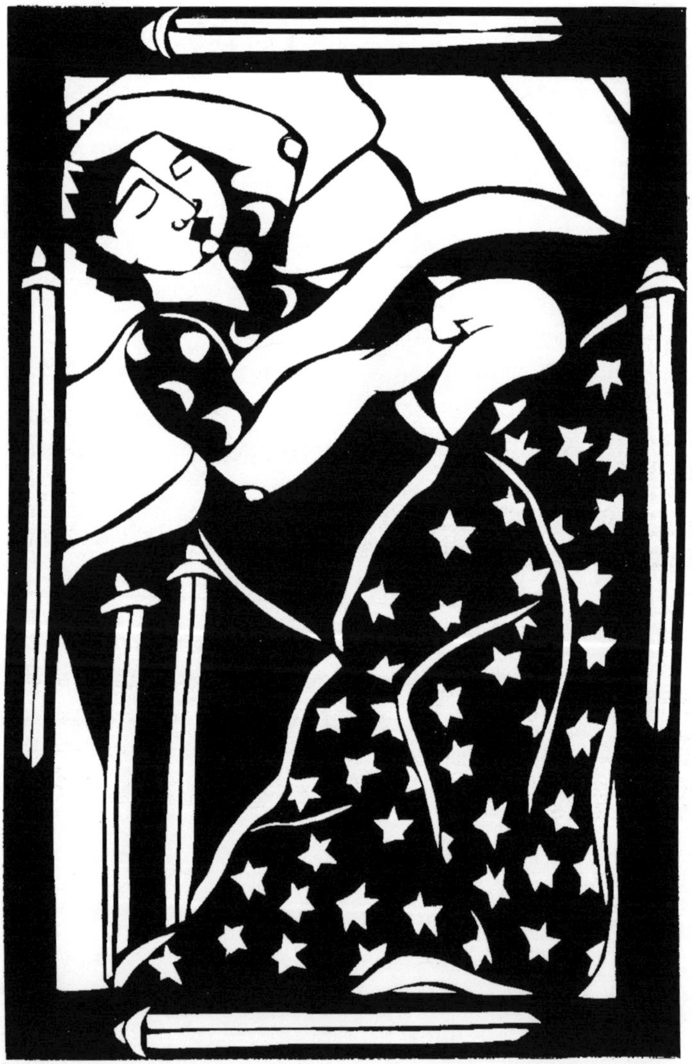

Six of Swords

rest through passage, a place of calm

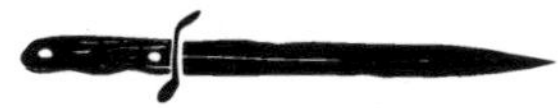

The figure in this image is dreaming beneath fabric covered in stars; she has moons on her top. Leaning back on a pillow, one hand is wrapped around her sleeping head while another is near the face of a cat who is curled up with her. While she is clearly resting, swords eerily surround her.

The Six of Swords ushers in transformation through calm. Times have been really complicated and taxing, but this card suggests that you have learned or will learn to internalize the pain without fighting it, and that your quiet acceptance of it will encourage movement through to the other side. It's a dark but gentle card, suggesting mourning or grief whose initial storm has passed. The feelings are still there, but they are less aggressive.

While this image depicts sleep, the card advocates for rest. On some level, in a reading this card invites you to actively but calmly internalize the struggle, rather than avoid it by sleeping through it. While the card indicates that you may have lately endured a substantial difficulty, it also points to the current balancing of emotions, some level of adjustment or harmony, and making it through.

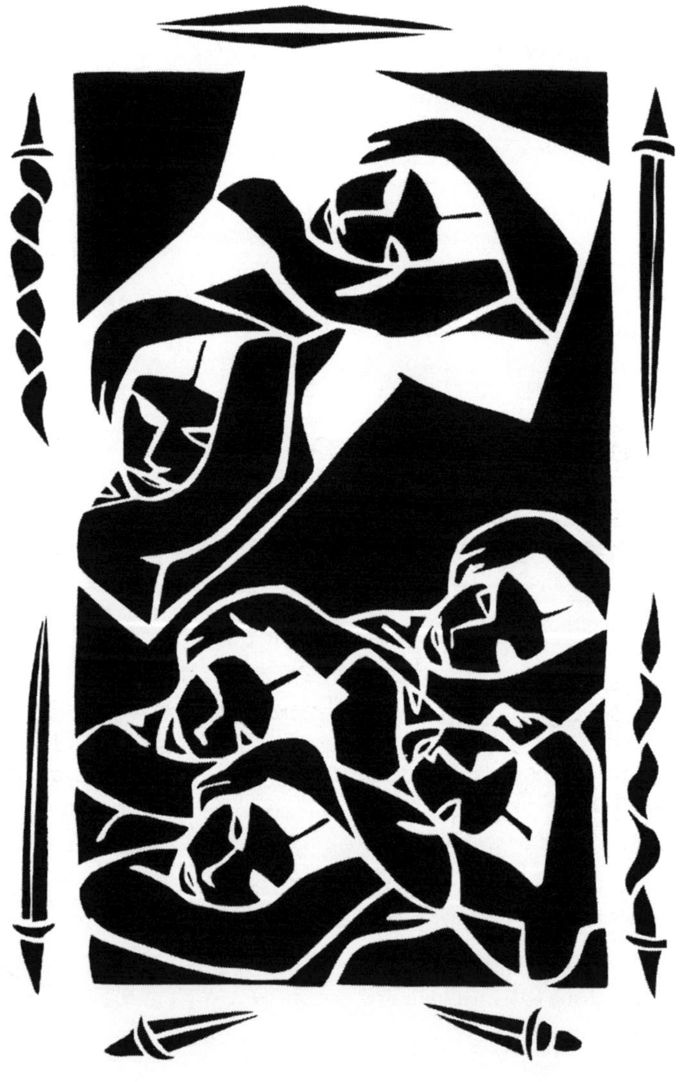

Seven of Swords

confusion, split energies, instability

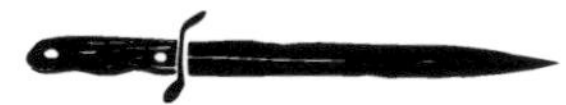

The image in this particular deck points to the possibility of community and support; it shows six people, lying together, all in the same protective pose.

There are a few possibilities here: The Seven can reveal overprotectiveness and a stubborn resistance to support; perhaps these individuals, though apparently intimate, are all privately struggling in spite of their proximity. That seems foolish, but it happens all the time! Sometimes we struggle to ask our neighbours or closest friends for help. And the card further carries the meaning of hypervigilance, suggesting that we may be scared of outsiders even when there is no current threat.

The other possibility in the Seven of Swords is that of evasiveness or underhanded, slapdash action. Ask yourself whether you've been quickly decisive in a way that alienates your closest people, when another option could have been to let them help you figure out your problem. And finally, there is the possibility of deceit, or not supplying or receiving all the facts when they are needed.

So overall the card in a reading strikes a balance between community and independence, truth and lies, and submission and protection. It urges you to reflect on what is needed in your particular situation. Often this card wants you to seek out support if you have not been doing so, or learn to act independently if you rarely do that.

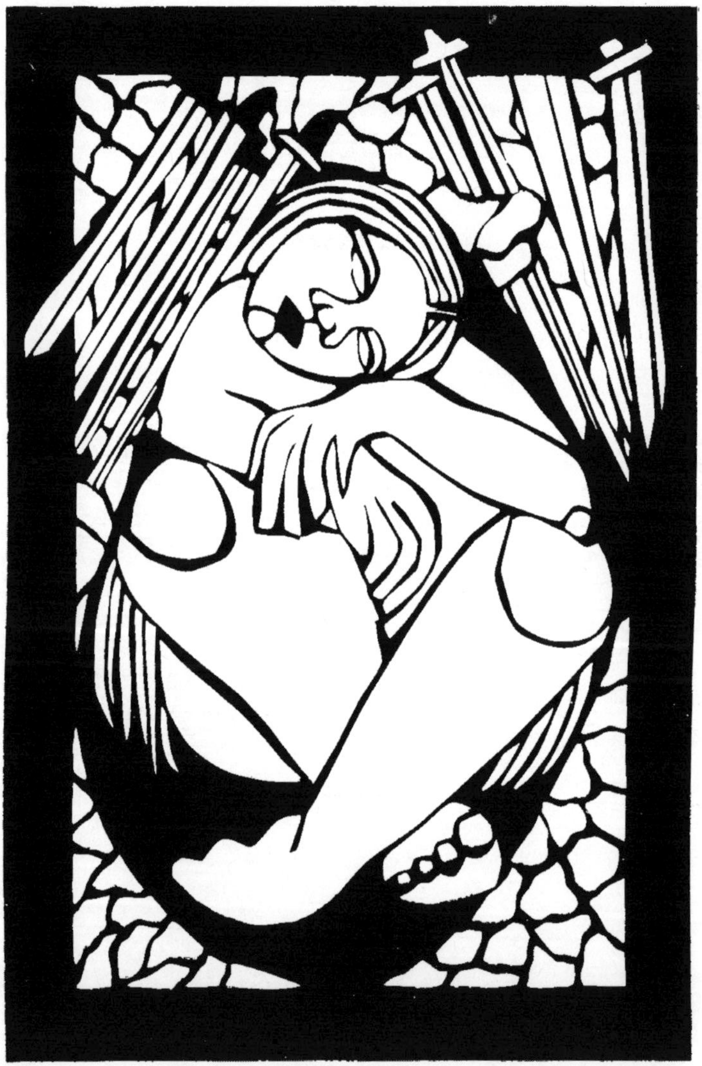

Eight of Swords

external pressure, introversion through crisis

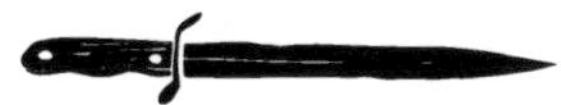

Trapped in an egg-shaped hole in a rock wall, this person bears a pile of swords on their shoulders. They are contorted into the smallest possible position, eyes closed or else rolled back, ankles and wrists crossed passively. They are enduring quietly.

This card portrays betrayal and entrapment, oppression even. It symbolizes an individual's complicity with or internalization of the circumstances that keep them restricted. Simultaneously, even within those conditions, it contains the possibility of release or relief from that position.

Because part of the immobility you may be experiencing lies in your own psyche, this card in a reading offers you a chance to recognize your participation in it as the beginning of a way out. Coping is necessary and has probably saved you from the true piercing of the swords lined up neatly beside your head, but this card also encourages you to eventually remove them—or at least increase the distance between you—through your own awareness of the conditions that are suppressing you.

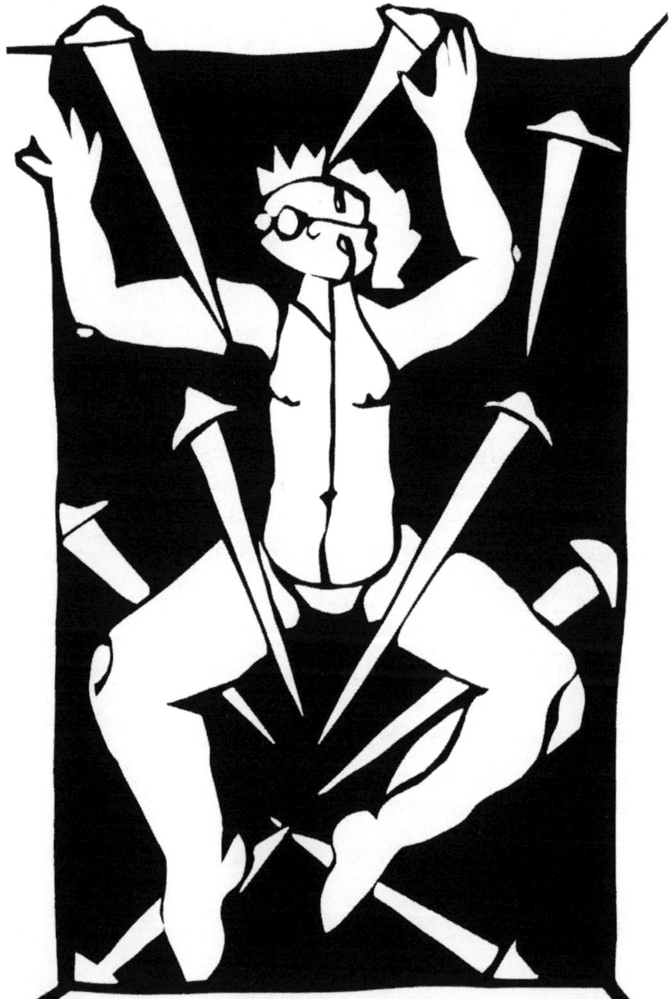

Nine of Swords

self-hate, indecision, suffering, despair

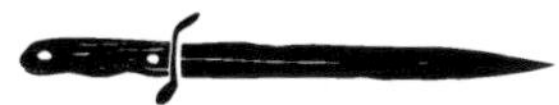

All of the swords in this image point at the central pained figure; they are placed all around her—one is even dangerously close to the side of her twisted head—but none of them have pierced her flesh.

While this card describes a moment of despair or ongoing draining external circumstances, it more importantly points to the self-harm, shame, and guilt that have become habitual because of the experience of pain, or anxiety layered from long-term oppression being released in response to something minor or unrelated. Sometimes the shame and nervous habits built up in response to challenging systemic circumstances are no longer serving you; these habits have passed the point of functioning as conscious coping and are increasingly leading to indecision and self-critique.

The Nine reminds you that circumstances will change. Or, if they don't, you could consider changing your responses to them, in order for them to serve your wellbeing. If you can in any way, be patient while things improve. Let your anxiety lift occasionally so that you can rest and get through this period without doing yourself more unnecessary harm. Those swords are not piercing you yet: try to take things as they come, and take care of yourself as you can.

If this card comes up in a reading, it may serve you to remind yourself that you are not currently in the danger you once were, to reflect on the ways you are hard on yourself when you feel threatened, and consider kinder methods of responding to your own pain.

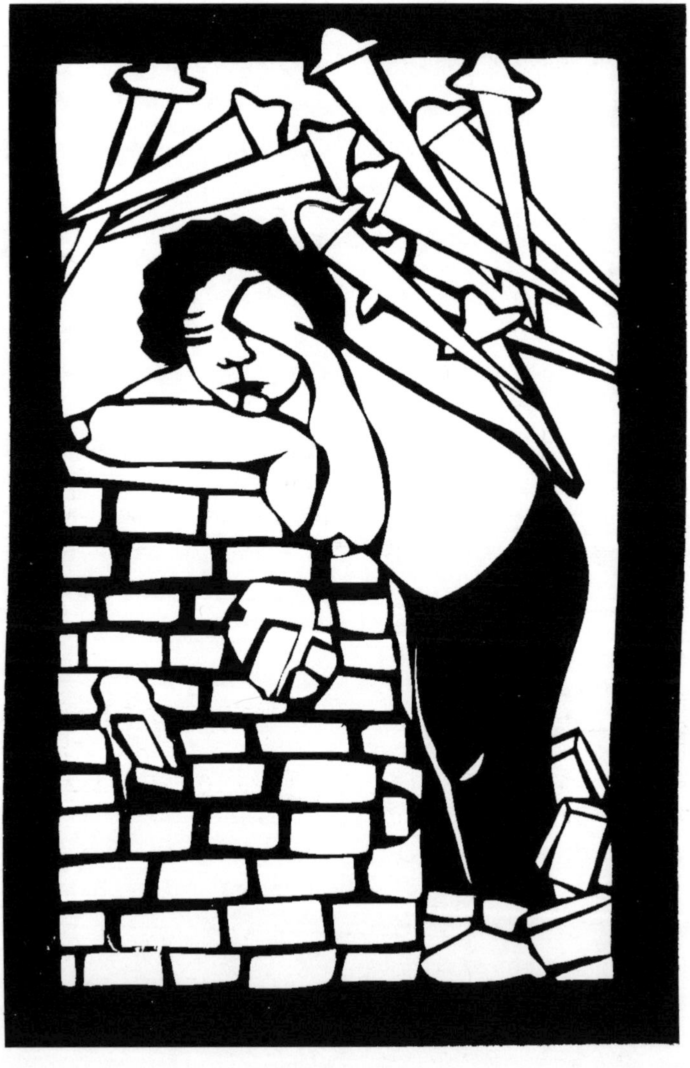

Ten of Swords

desolation, ruin, defeat, delusion

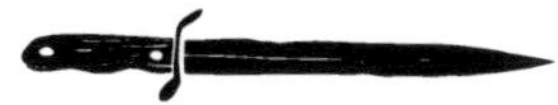

This card quite clearly depicts despair. It takes one sword to hurt, but here there are ten, piled on top of a single person with their own fist clamped in sorrow over their eye, leaning on a broken wall. Things are rough.

The extreme amount of swords can, in some situations, point to hysteria—a reaction triggered by relatively minor events. In others, it can be quite literal. Here is pain, tragedy, and loss of hope. There are ways out of this experience. Despair can be alleviated by some calm, distraction, time.

In a situation in which you are reacting strongly or uncontrollably, think about whether there are ways in which your reaction is increasing your suffering. Are your feelings related to past events? They can be real and heavy in response to fleeting experiences, and also in response to long-term, oppressive ones. If you are in pain because of a hardship or tragedy, this card asks you to seek some support to eventually lead to healing. It won't always feel this bad, but it truly does now.

In a reading, the Ten of Swords wants you to think about how you are feeling in relation to how events have objectively played out—feelings of betrayal and injustice can allow you to accumulate wisdom and do it differently next time. Beginning to parse apart the triggers and loss, while honouring the pain and moving through feelings of defeat, can bring some closure to the swords' cycle of despair and conflict.

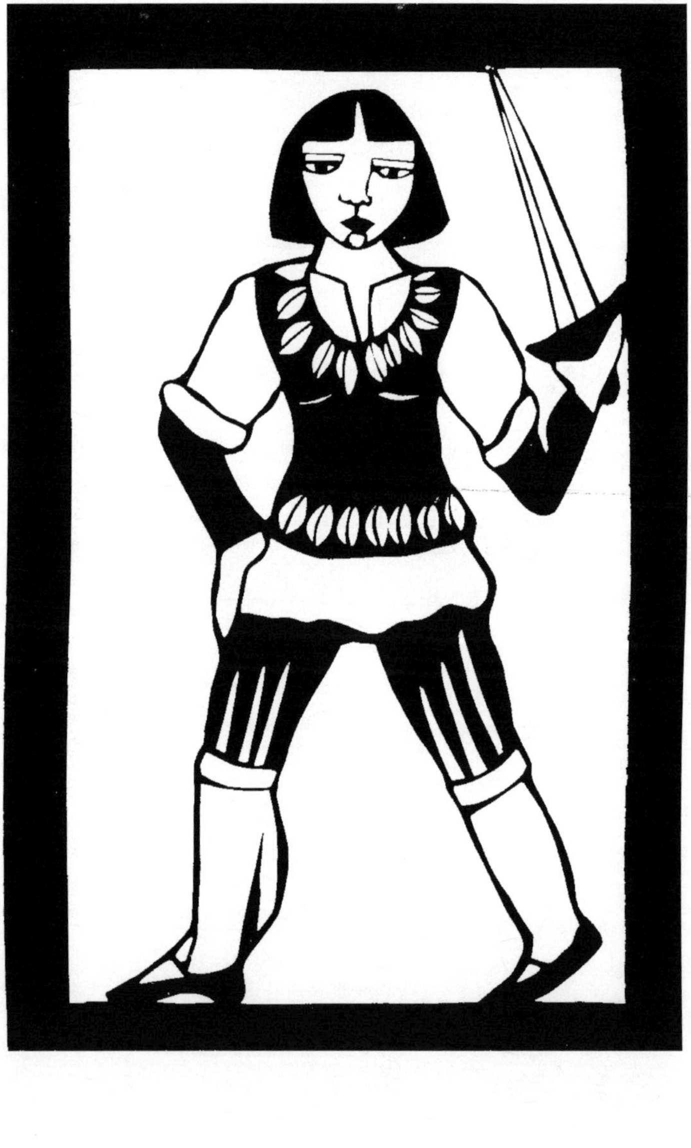

Child of Swords

diligence, power, attraction, initiation

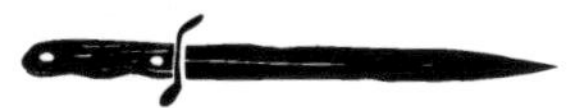

Gently stepping across the frame, dressed for battle, this Child is hardly threatening. There is little resolve in that stance, but a lot of detail on the outfit. The person is clearly putting energy into something, and it's probably not the fight they could be having.

As all swords are, this Child is largely associated with clear thinking and communication, and asserting boundaries. But as all Children are, this Sword is still learning. As the messenger of the suit ruling the mind, the Child of Swords testifies to your access to the power of clearly passing on information.

In a reading, this card suggests a light, perhaps flippant, approach to interpersonal friction. Depending on your situation, this approach can reduce your anxiety if it tends to verge on disproportionate. However, the card also asks you to think about whether you're dealing sufficiently with conflict.

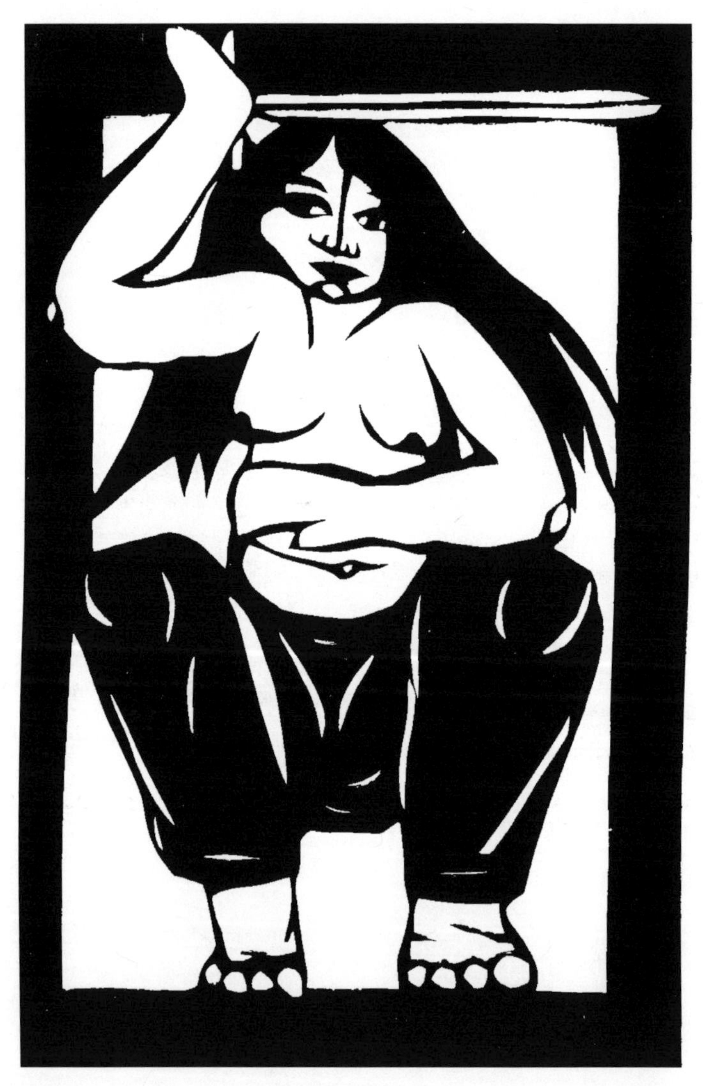

SWORD AMAZON

moment, force impetuousness, impressionability

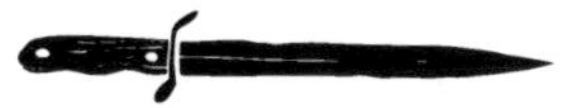

So here's someone squatting tensely, ready to leap up shirtless and fling that sword. Her heels are up; her hair is flying. She's brave, and she's also a bit foolish, in the reckless way of Amazons generally. This is the Gemini of the deck, all twins and flirting and chatting.

The Amazon in the air suit signifies that impetuousness, impromptu generosity, and quick and maybe careless defence are at play. You're going to fling that sword across the room before you look who's there, or step in between someone and the person they're about to punch, even though they would have rather carried through with it. It's that sudden movement before you've thought about the consequences, an uproar before a discussion even happens, falling off the sidewalk because you didn't see the pothole while in the middle of conversation.

This card turning up in a reading might help support you when you need a quick and fearless approach—you'll tell it like it is—and damage you for similar reasons. Your wit and insight are necessary right now, and it might work out in your favour to use them wisely.

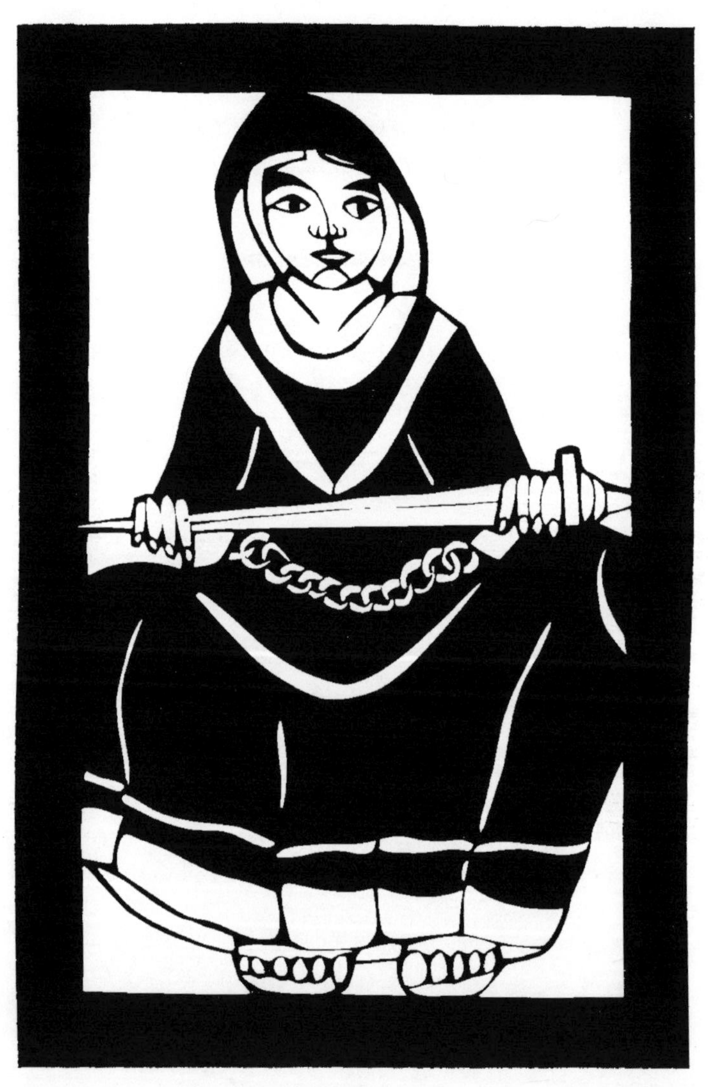

Daughter of Swords

fair, good counsel, sure-footed, reserved

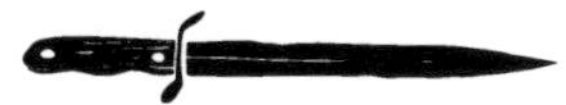

With a firm clutch on a sharp object, the Daughter of Swords has gained wisdom through pain. In a sense a Minor Arcana Justice, and like her zodiacal associate Aquarius, she speaks fairly and honestly, piercing through clouds of confusion to voice a cold, glistening truth.

Representing you or someone influential, this person is probably an ice queen, who reasons through all your sensitivities and brings them out glistening and more static than they were. She is also strong, and burdened and heavy with reason, and able to cut through the bullshit. She has lived through so much, and trusts her analysis and self-sufficiency more than anything, because they have been instrumental in her survival.

With this card appearing in a reading, you may lack a basic level of kindness and care. Your experiences of loss, pain, and scarcity have made you powerful and independent, deeply self-aware and smart. It could be wise to put a little warmth into your honest and sometimes harsh words, because even when you are speaking the hard truth, people may hear it better if it is wrapped in something resembling love.

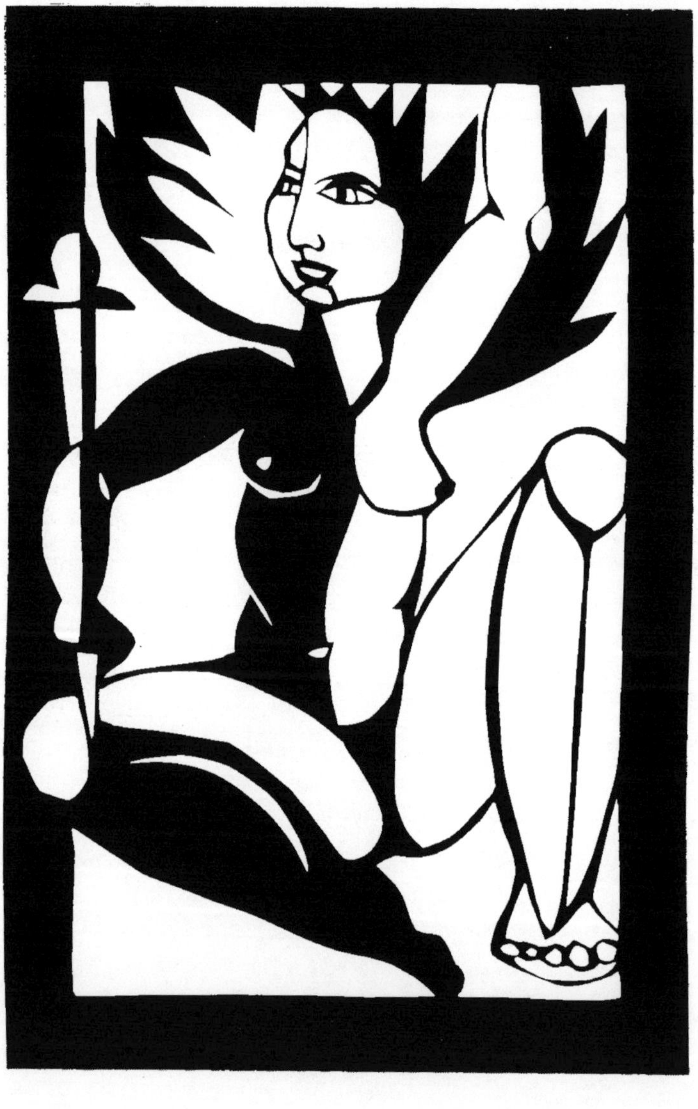

Sword Mother

authority, initiative, intelligence, centre of air

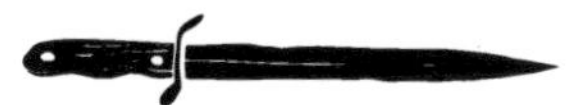

While this figure is seated, she does not appear to be seated on anything. The Sword Mother prioritizes intellect and wisdom above other things, as well as the ability to remain on that level while people play out their emotional, material, or passionate skirmishes below. She is aloof and exudes authority. This is the card associated with Libra, who while social is driven fundamentally by truth and intellect more than by feelings.

The Sword Mother promotes the application of fair principles to real-world problems, carrying out ideologically sound yet sensible plans. She can also inspire remoteness, to the point of an inability to feel or even demonstrate compassion for your human surroundings. This most mature representative of the suit of intellect needs grounding in the other elements of the deck not to float too far away from compassion, passion, and sensuality.

Look at that far-off gaze, that upright sword, her other arm held high and her hair floating up with her into the world of the mind. In a reading, she can represent a domineering and hyperrational authority or someone driven by ideals, truth, and justice—or else your own movement in one of those directions.

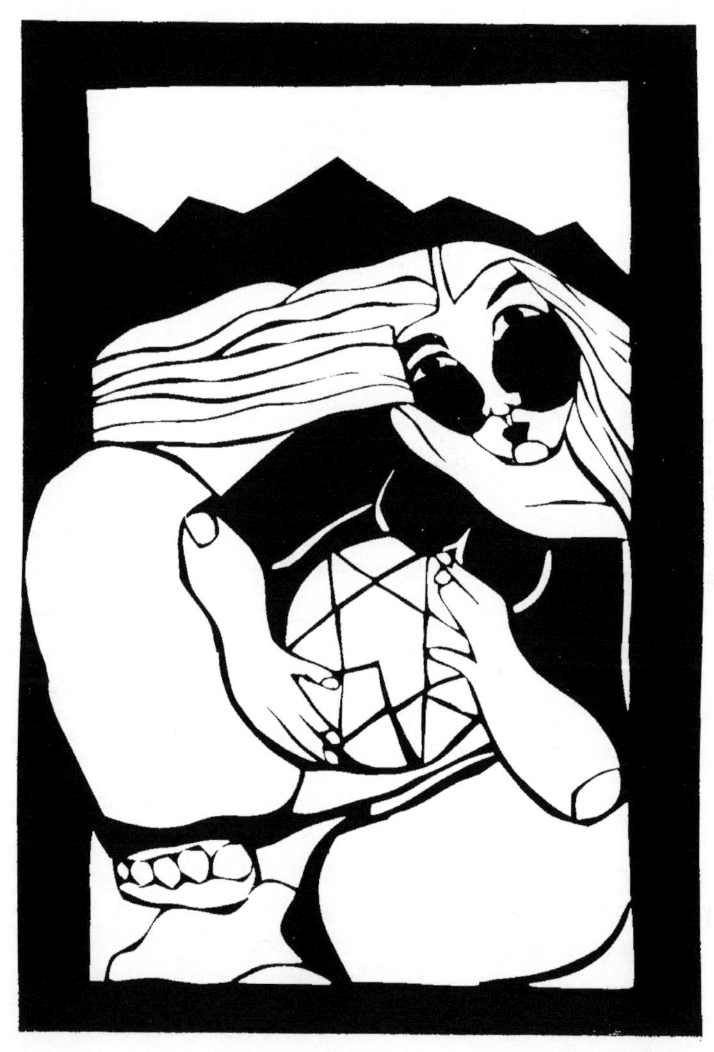

Ace of Pentacles

prosperity, material wellbeing, security

This cool guy is blissed out, hair flying but parted neatly, a giant pentacle held in their angular embrace, their bare legs and feet drawn up around it as well, holding it in, enjoying it.

In the Ace of Pentacles we discover the gifts of the physical, the sensual, the earth, security, and material wealth. You're on your way, you have the opportunity, embrace it. It's pretty cool to find that you have what you need and want. With this Ace you have the possibility of getting it—a job, a new garden, some special gift or book or cheque or garment you've been waiting for. With the Ace of Pentacles, in particular, there's the possibility of detrimentally overstocking, greedily hoarding. Or, if you have what you need, not noticing it.

In a reading, this card suggests that you can get what you need, and that you pay attention to what you've got, holding it gently but firmly in your hands, pursing your lips in joy and gratitude.

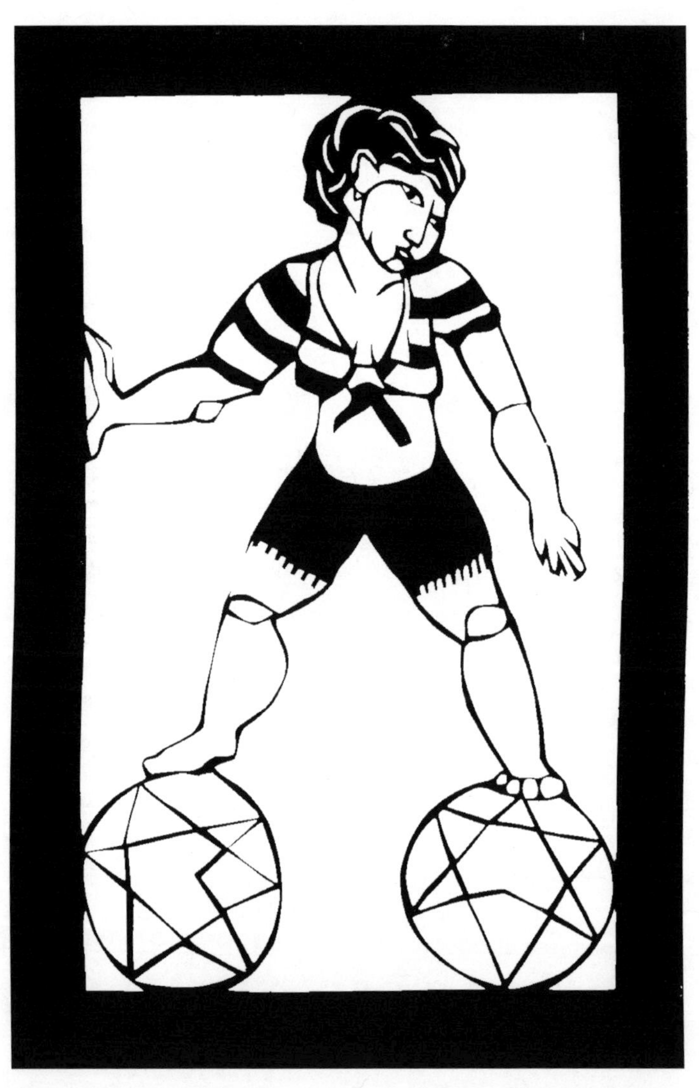

Two of Pentacles

polarity, change, agility, and harmony

In cut-offs with her shirt tied under her boobs, this person has one hand balanced against the wall, each foot on a giant pentacle. Her neck looks a little crunched, perhaps. She's pulling it off, but it's hard to balance that much for that long.

This card can suggest a couple things: One is that you have to make up your mind. Choose a pentacle—you have so many options, and you're spending a lot of energy keeping all of them balanced, both feet off the ground, scattered and shaky. Another is that you've managed to juggle and balance so well that your efforts have come to fruition. You've worked with your resources in such a way that they are blossoming for you. Your perseverance is remarkable.

Regardless, where you find this card in a reading, your flexibility and optimism are helpful for either coming to a decision or figuring out how to make the best use of your creative resources. In the earth suit, the reward could be finding magic in ordinary pleasures or finding grace in your effectiveness—cut-offs, kink in your neck, and all.

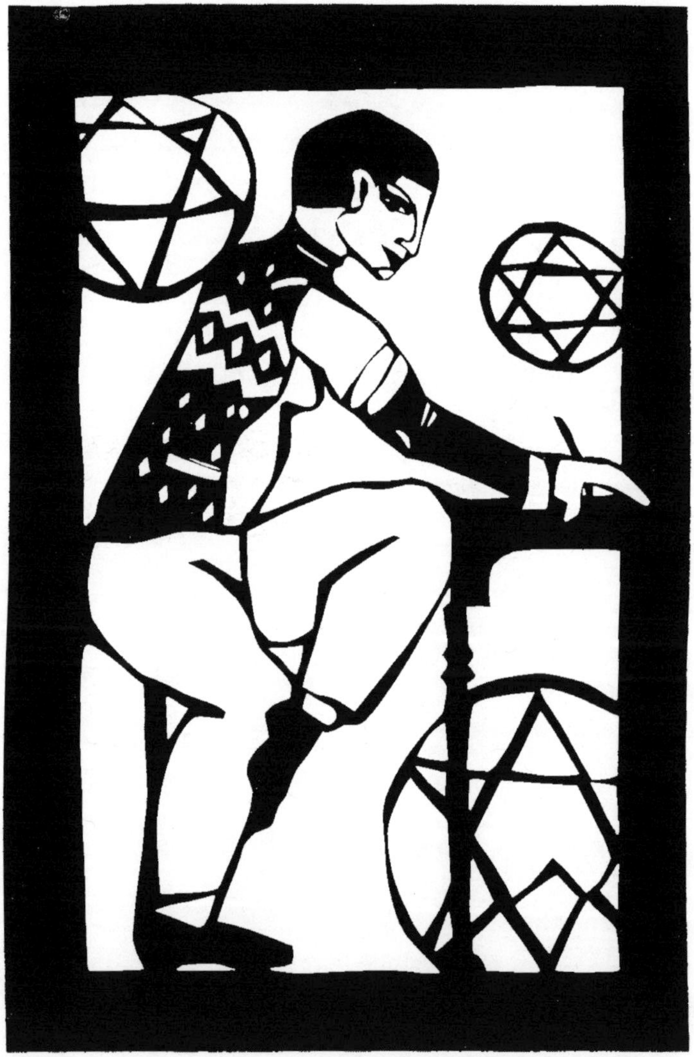

Three of Pentacles

constructive, practical, material, self-willed

This fey character is sitting at her desk, one poofy-pantsed leg crossed over the other. Large pentacles hover around her desk and patterned sweater. Her hair is cut straight across the back of the neck, classic barber-shop style. Here the pentacles, as with all threes, are at their finest: she is working; her labour is useful and also profoundly meaningful; she is dapper; the legs of her table are well shaped. She has in her possession what she values, and she also finds the magic in absorbing herself in the ways in which she values herself.

This card suggests that not only is your work valuable, but it has led to your self-development and self-awareness. You may be contributing to your communities in ways that work for you, and also in ways that are valuable to them: through your hard work. And—if you're anything like this guy—your good fashion. Not to mention your sense of physicality and play indicated by the pose you strike.

If you pull this card, take a look at the work in your life / your life's work. Are you enjoying what you do for a living? Are you determined to finish the projects that you want or need to do? Do you push yourself too hard and lose sight of the value and meaning in what you labour at? Here is work's most delightful balance of body, mind, and spirit, firmly rooted in life's struggles, and contributing to the beauty, function, and rewards of what you and yours value.

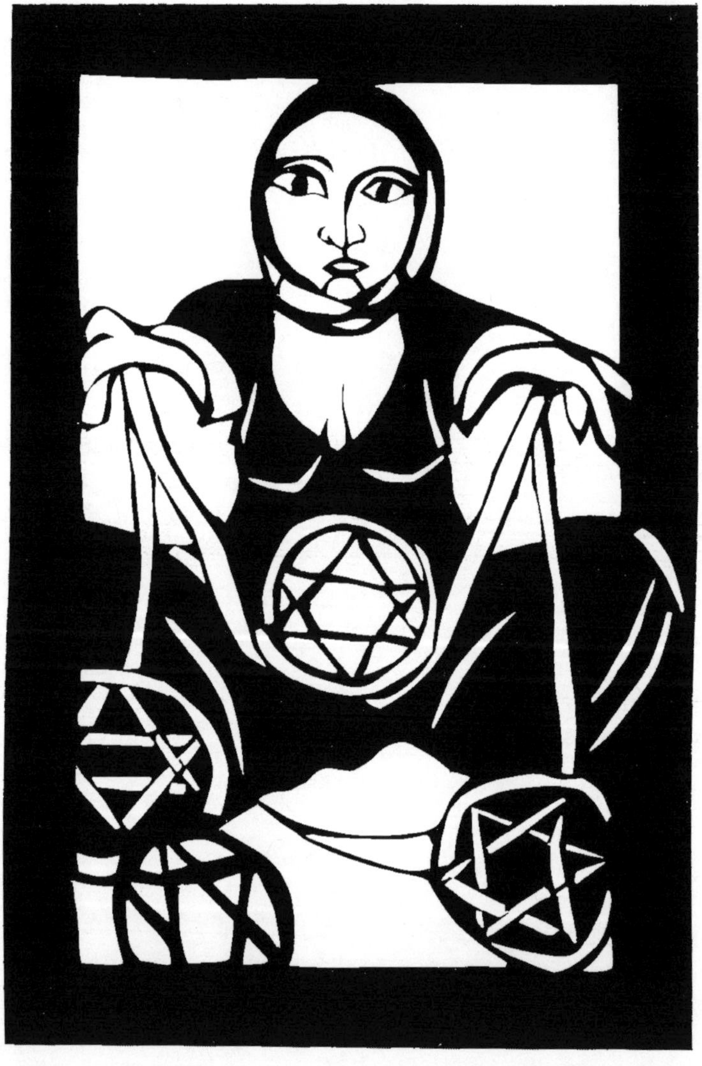

Four of Pentacles

orderly, settled, crafty, financially capable

Look at the concentration in that face, the dexterity in those hands, that careful rope of pentacles staying above the ground. The figure in this card undermines herself with her own restrictive nature. She can clearly balance life's practical matters—money, work, daily routines, the materials of her trade or craft—but sometimes she struggles with relaxing or feeling anything through all the structure that surrounds her.

When emotional energy gets too leaky, being organized and even selfish materially can help it be regathered or reabsorbed. On the other hand, trying to contain or monitor your emotions through material collection—saving money, creating a comfortable home, collecting cans of beans for the apocalypse—doesn't protect against damage with certainty. In fact, as with any of the suits, if you're too focused on the accumulation and ordering of stuff, as is the case with the Four of Pentacles, you may lose the ability to face the other realms of life with practice and ability.

When this card comes up in a reading, think about whether you are being selfish, and why. Has everything recently been taken away from you because you were so generous, and now you are trying to right the balance, in order that you have something? Are you trying to contain your emotional life (or even give yourself the semblance of one) with money, crafts, or other physical things? If you have a room full of sweaters, consider whether the other parts of your existence (the feelings, passion, and rationality of the three other suits) are being neglected by this extreme accumulation and focus.

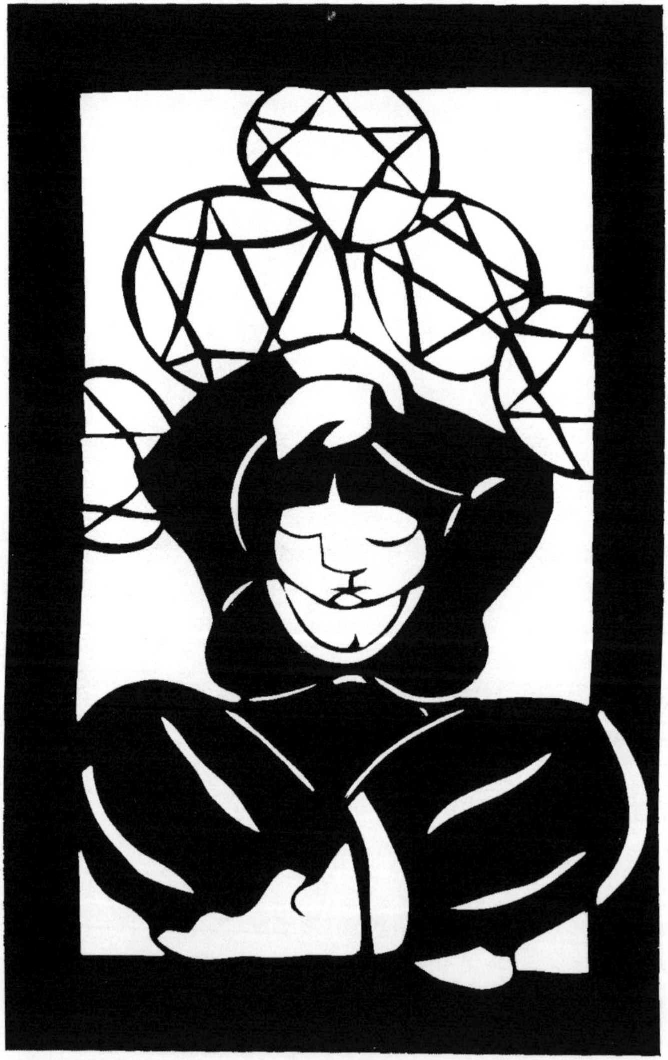

Five of Pentacles

insecurity, introversion due to stress

Here is someone burdened by coins. She is cross-legged, slouched with her breasts touching her knees, hands over her head to protect it from the weight from above. Her eyes are closed. It's too much.

She is someone who has been feeling scarcity for too long, whether as a response to her situation of lack, out of anxiety around resources, or a little bit of both. In any case, it's really weighing on her. It might be self-destruction, or it might be the burdens of capitalism, but she's been in survival mode and has trouble seeing room for alternatives or the people or institutions around her who might be able to provide support. Or maybe they just aren't there.

The Five of Pentacles is a call for community care and self-care. You have a right to fulfil your basic needs, and to not give away so much of yourself that you can't. You also have a right to support and generosity from those who surround you.

When you get this card in a reading, look around a little. It's so so hard, when you're just surviving, to see the possibilities or the ways the things you can access could finally break open a new less lacking life. In any case, your scarcity or fear of it might actually be destroying you—your sense of home, your relationships, your health. And this Five suggests it would be worth trying to see some opportunity in the resources and communities around you, though your head is hung so low you might miss them. Look up for a moment when you can.

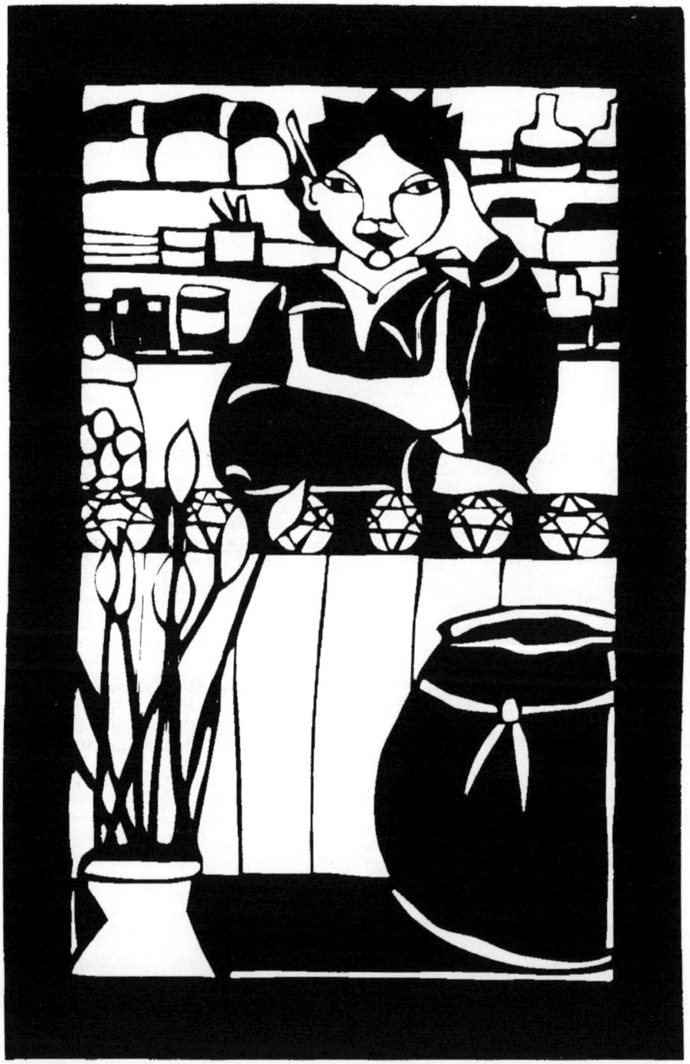

Six of Pentacles

good fortune, brief material success

This engaging person with a pen behind her ear stands at a busy and well-organized service counter, ready to get you what you want.

The simultaneous meanings of personal success and balance in relationships are wrapped up in this card. They are related in that they both ask us as individuals to provide for others what they need (which may differ from their expressions of what they need); to value ourselves in order to ask for what we need; and to strive to attain those needs rather than sacrificing resources we hardly have or our personal aspirations.

More intricately, the Six of Pentacles looks at relationships where power is distributed unequally. Dominance/submission, charity, and inherently unbalanced familial relationships are possibilities here. In a reading, you're asked to reflect on where you're giving and receiving in an imbalanced way, and from within those relationships, to figure out if you're being as generous as you can, receiving graciously, and fulfilling your own giving and receiving needs.

This card's position in a reading shows where you may be receiving advice or nourishment from someone who has power over you, or where you hold such power. This could be a consensual arrangement, or it could be an insidious power imbalance that you may not have recognized as such. This card coaxes you to seek success based on self-value, to have your needs fulfilled, and to provide for others without shame.

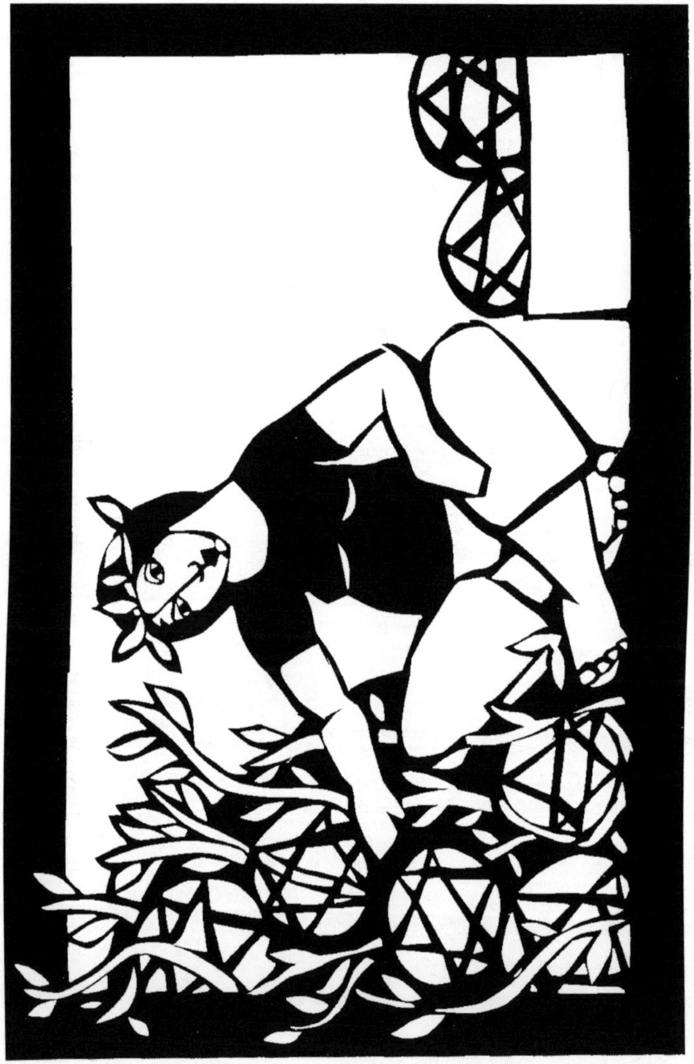

Seven of Pentacles

sowing, cultivation, results with physical labour

The woman in this image sits looking toward the pentacles she is extracting from the brambles in order to add them to the pile next to her. The ones in the box beside her are unmonitored, out of her line of sight, yet she is secure in the knowledge that they are still there. The horizontal orientation of the card contributes to the firmness of something built and something being built upon depicted side by side.

This card demonstrates the satisfying outcome of persistent efforts. At this point in your labours, the process has been long and consistent enough that you can count on its yields having a life that exists beyond your direct input.

The fruits of labour, the rewards of a sustained project—this card in a reading suggests that your work is paying off. You can relax for a moment while the results of your efforts go on, self-sustaining. You may have also hit a decisive turning point—whether to back away from those brambles to go grow a new bush and let them keep growing on their own, or to stay tending them, building them up even further.

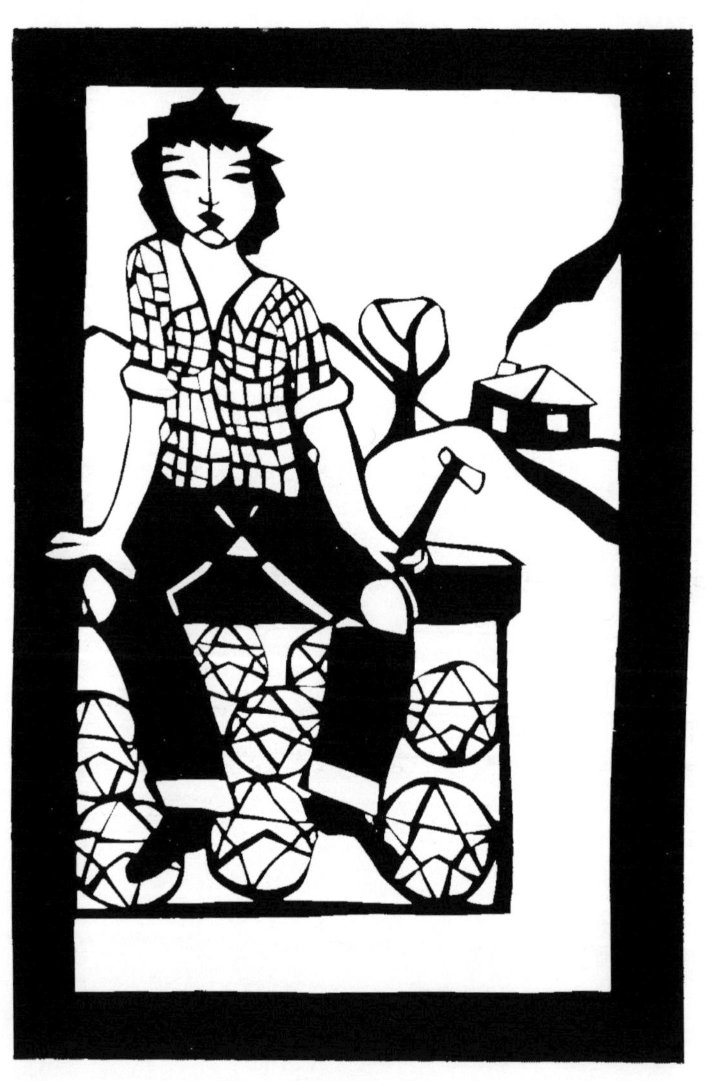

Eight of Pentacles

energy gathering, building, making crafts

Look at this guy, sitting on a solid box she just built, sleeves rolled up, thinking of home but wanting to finish her project before she goes back there. She is lost in her work, with a process-based ethic rather than a motivating desire for the end result.

This card evidences patience and discipline regarding a task, suggesting that building steadily on natural skills can be rewarding in itself but also eventually lead to material security and pride in achievement, two foundational drives of the pentacles suit.

Apprenticeship or focus on tasks can also be isolating, though, and this Eight, when it appears in a reading, also asks you to make sure the work you're doing is rooted in your communities' needs. Even if you have to make something in solitude, it will only be satisfying if it fulfils a larger purpose. For now, though, just keep working. That box of pentacles is almost full. Your little hatchet is staying sharp; the fireplace at home has been lit; your hair is scattered with the sweat of labour. Just keep working on that shit, it's looking good.

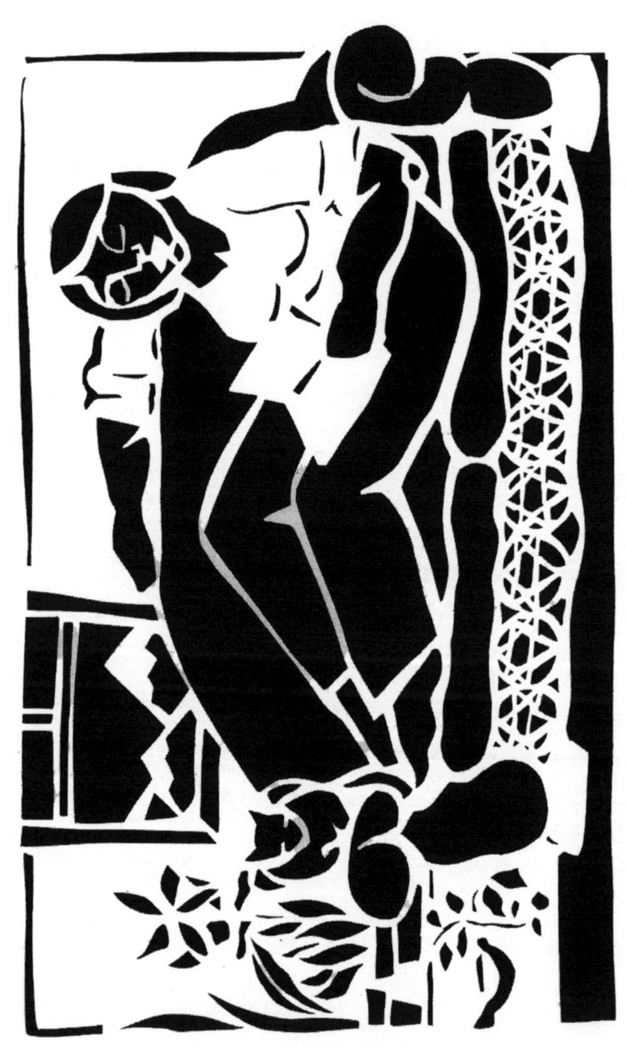

Nine of Pentacles

gains, harvest, good fortune, finished work

Lounging on the couch, reading, this person lies with a cat at her feet. A thriving potted lily blooms. Her face is calm, her eyes downturned. Her couch has a base of woven coins. The horizontal image suggests expansiveness. Cognizant of her wealth, she is truly revelling in the material and physical comfort she has worked for and is blessed with.

Potential and hard work and success and bounty—these are all qualities of the Nine of Pentacles. But more so, in being close to the end of one cycle of growth, the harvest and abundance of this card are meant to fill you with pleasure. Its meanings also include some level of compromise—to fulfil a need for discipline, self-sufficiency, and success in pursuit of goals, some level of loneliness or at least self-reliance is necessary. Your cat is a loving companion, though.

In a reading, the Nine of Pentacles challenges you to feel good about what you have, how well things are working, the support of your community, and the richness—wherever you can find it—in your life.

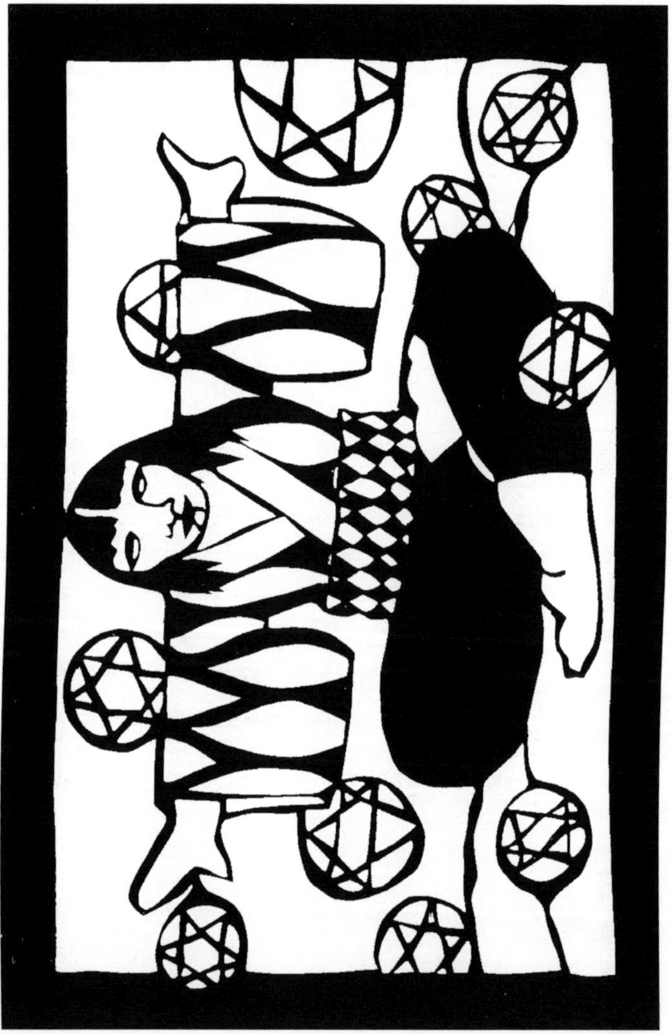

Ten of Pentacles

established comfort, gathering in of past knowledge

Surrounded by pentacles, seated on what appears to be rolling hills or a pile of pillows or blankets, draped in patterned clothing, this person reaches her arms out beyond her peripheral vision to amass the floating coins that surround her. For the most part she is strangely unaware of them.

This is a card of abundance. The Ten of Pentacles sometimes lacks awareness of this wealth, though, and it asks us to evaluate what we possess, and to consider whether we are denying our potential resources or taking pleasure in what we have and sharing that wealth.

If you are securely established, the card suggests you pay attention to that, to share and experience the security in having something that supports you and those you care for. If your resources are meagre or unstable, or if you have been experiencing a lowered quality of life, the Ten of Pentacles implores you to examine how this could be tied up to restrictions from your family and to relationships that have to shift in order for you to create prosperity, whatever that means, with the resources you have. Regardless of the situation, the symbolism of security and harmony is something to either celebrate or strive for in order to lay a foundation.

If you get this card in a reading, aim to be patient with yourself emotionally, generous on the whole, and aware of the magic in the everyday. If things seem to be going well, it's worth taking pleasure in what you have been able to create for your communities and family.

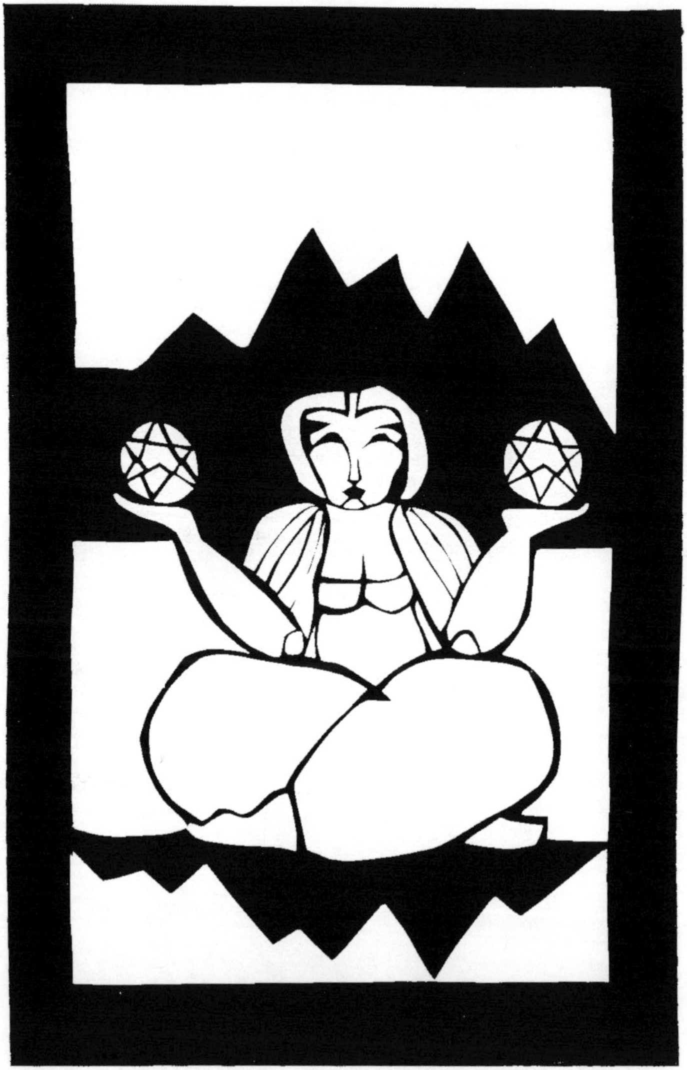

Child of Pentacles

solid, diligent, psychic, lover of the earth

Look at that haggard, sombre face, those jagged mountains, those ballooning pants. Pentacles are in part about work, which shows in this figure's face; solidity or groundedness, which shows in their seated position; and in beautiful things, which shows in their curated outfit.

Here is the student, applying their diligence to the mountains of knowledge behind them, learning or doing for their own sake and not for the reward. The mountains need to be there as a subject of study. The doggedness, the focus, the seated determination can overwhelm you without direction. You can get a bruised bum from discipline regarding your seatedness; you can apply your diligence to endless consumption and black out; you can become a student of restricting your enjoyment of food.

In a reading, this Child shows where you may find nascent projects, talents, ideas, or messages that, given time and some restraint, will produce something of earthly value.

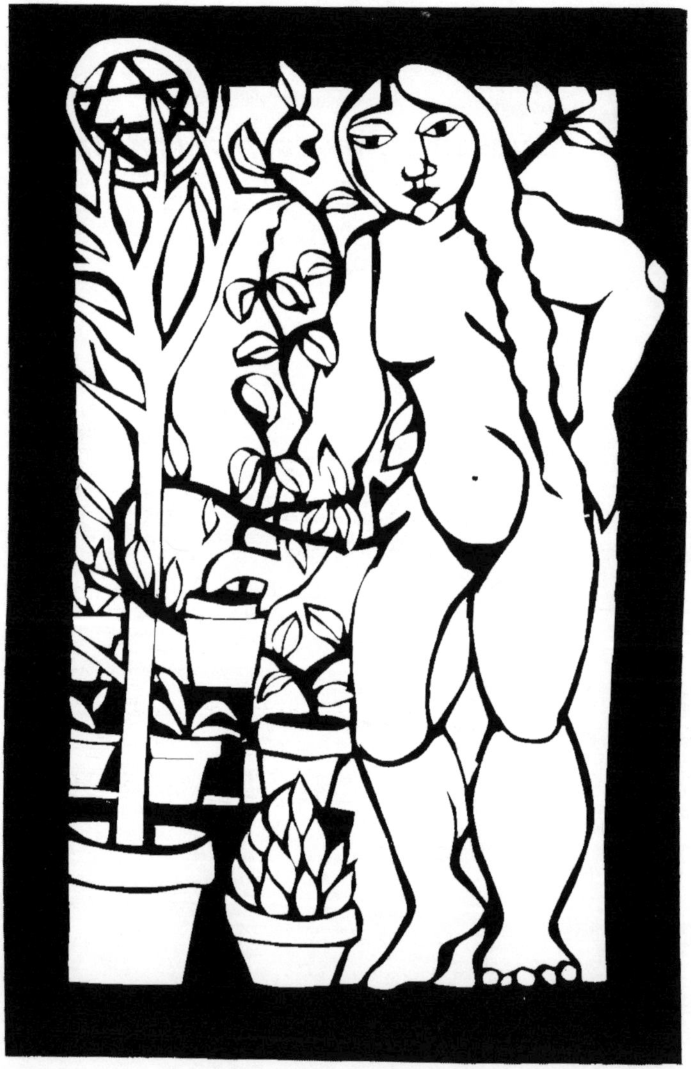

Pentacle Amazon

practical, productive, keeper of food and shelter

Hand on her hip, naked, her eyes gazing at the sea of potted greenery in front of her, this Amazon is detail oriented like Virgo, her astrological twin. Pierced on the branch of a tree is a pentacle, out of reach. She's so focused on the growth of those plants that she's forgotten the whereabouts of those other valuable things.

In this card we find growth and structure—gardening, in the case of this deck. The potential fault in this Amazon lies in her tenacity. She's just a-growing things. She's not necessarily sure why. The production isn't laden with meaning, emotion, or analysis for her, as it would be in the other suits—she's just doing it. Maybe it reduces her anxiety. In any case, like a Virgo, she's a good workhorse, so unselfishly devoted to the task and to giving. The Amazonian qualities combined with the pentacle practicality ensure that.

If this card comes up in a reading, it might be worth thinking about what you're working so hard at. Why? Does it make you feel good? Is it mentally stimulating? Is it intuitively or meaningfully enriching? If it's not, turn away from the details of your garden for a little minute and try to balance those other elements. If you realize you don't want to be doing it at all, stop it. Let the person you're working for tend their own garden, or start your own.

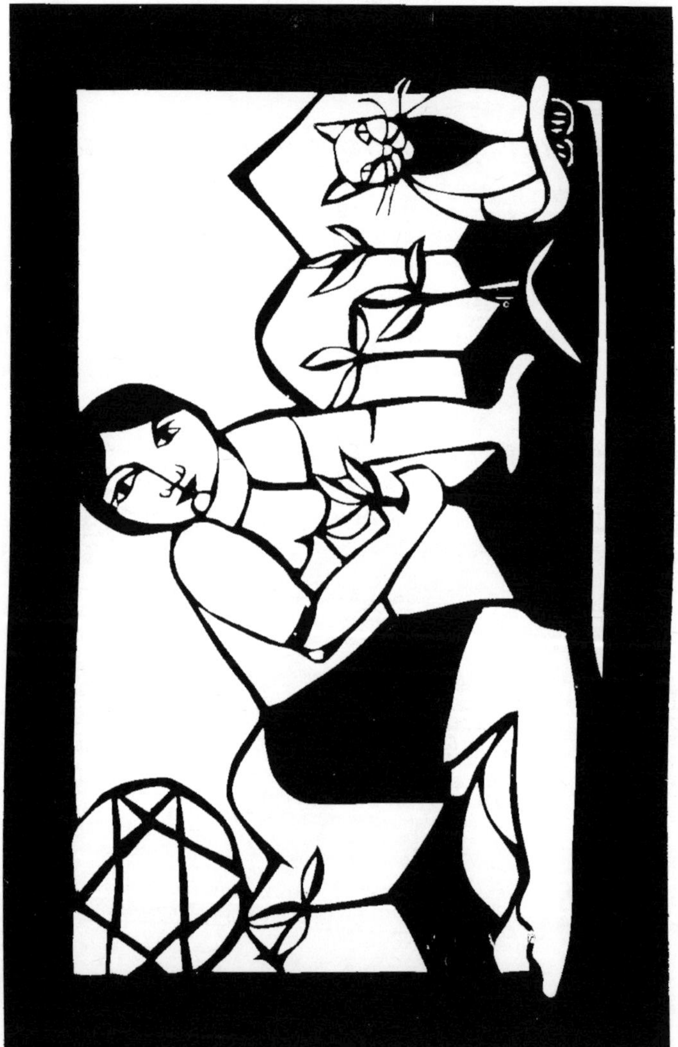

Daughter of Pentacles

systematic, persevering, balanced, prudent

Here is the queen of beautiful things, surrounded by her garden, kneeling on the earth, a cat near her fingertips. The sun is a pentacle above the mountains behind her. Like Taurus, her astrological sister, she is contented and still.

She is someone who is deeply aware of what she possesses, as well as her own skills and values. She is rooted in reality and the magic of the material. She is generous, domestic, compassionate, and probably good with money. Look at that expanse of card! She truly is living a good life; but she's also extremely responsible.

This card's placement in a reading denotes ambition and wellbeing. It can represent someone supporting you, but also encouraging your self-determination and self-reliance. Or you may be cultivating these qualities in yourself: security, awareness, rootedness.

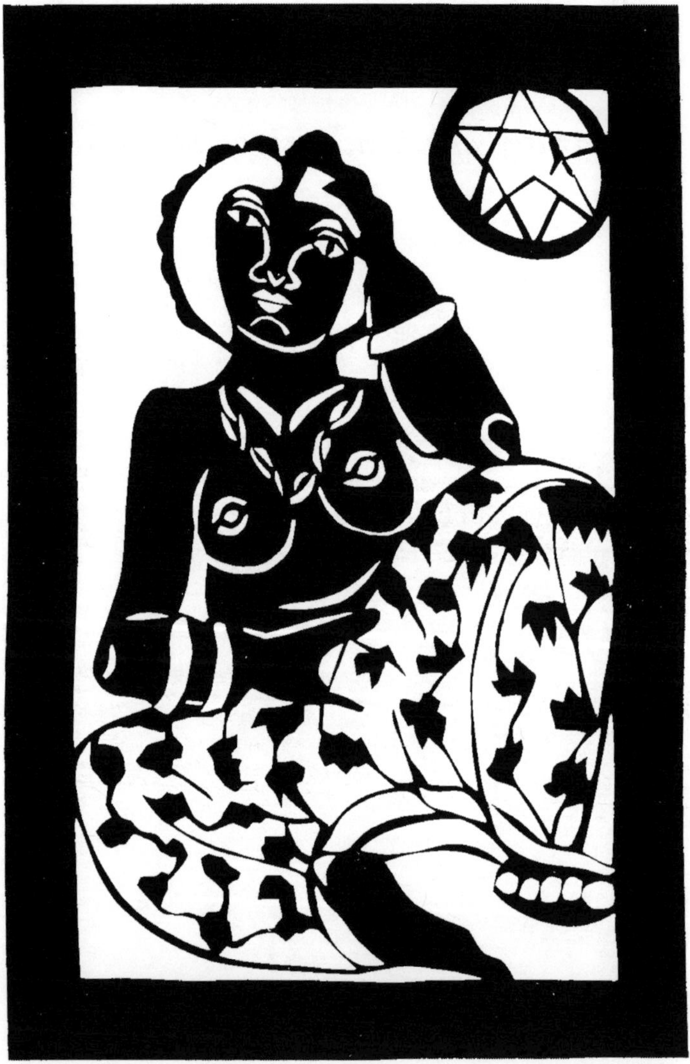

Pentacle Mother

fertility, affection, spirit of the earth

This woman is seated, content, with a serious face. She's thoughtful—one hand rests against the side of her head. She has nice necklaces and pants. Like Capricorn, her associated astrological sign, she has it all, but she is restrained in her success.

The Pentacle Mother is responsible—having achieved success through persistence, she expects others to do the same. Sometimes she may be a little cool or uncreative, but ideally this card suggests a mastery of creativity, success in an artistic field, or generally a firm and thoughtful hold on resources and materials. Overall, however, this person is responsible and sure-footed, thinking and feeling slowly and maturely.

When you get this card in a reading, it bodes well for your material success, persistence, and restraint. You are working toward something, perhaps living a more drab or rule-burdened life than you have in the past, but getting there—because like a Capricorn, your goal is to get there, to that height and out of the fray, where you can finally rest and take some kind of sedate pleasure in what you have gained.

Bios

Oliver Pickle is a Montreal-based trans writer, publisher, and editor with a soft spot for the esoteric and supernatural. Long-committed to tarot for the skeptical and unconvinced, Oliver leans toward contemporary readings of tarot, often re-visioned through a feminist, queer, and trans lens. Oliver's work has also appeared in *The Collection: Short Fiction from the Transgender Vanguard*, *make/shift* magazine, and other publications.

Ruth West, after graduating with a degree in art, created Thea's Tarot in 1984 in papercut, based on Billy Potts' *A New Women's Tarot*. Since then, she has become an internationally recognized artist working with digital art. One of the first graduates with a Master's of Fine Arts in Computer Graphics, Ruth West's art has grown steadily along with this medium. She was the first computer artist in residence at Monet's Garden in Giverny, France, creating an 80-piece series called the *Digital Garden*. Her work can be seen at ruthwest.com.

Rima Athar is a lover and a fighter with roots in Pakistan and connections to feminist organizing for rights and justice all over the world. You will most likely catch her on an adventure, revelling in nature and beauty, swept up in thought, laughing under the moon, stretching on a mountaintop, making use of her hands, swimming in the ocean, and shape-shifting a lot.

Also Available from Metonymy Press

Dear Twin
Addie Tsai

Little Blue Encyclopedia (for Vivian)
Hazel Jane Plante

nîtisânak
Lindsay Nixon

Lyric Sexology Vol. 1
Trish Salah

Fierce Femmes and Notorious Liars: A Dangerous Trans Girl's Confabulous Memoir
Kai Cheng Thom

Small Beauty
jiaqing wilson-yang

Resources

The Collective Tarot, *The Collective Tarot: A Magical Collaboration*, Portland, OR: Eberhardt Press, 2009.

Rachel Pollack, *Seventy-Eight Degrees of Wisdom: A Book of Tarot*, San Francisco, CA: Red Wheel/Weiser, 2007 (first edition 1980).

Billie Potts, *A New Women's Tarot*, Woodstock, NY: Elf and Dragons Press, 1978 (first edition 1977).

Juliet Sharman-Burke and Liz Greene, *The Mythic Tarot*, New York, NY: Simon & Schuster, 2001 (first edition 1986).

Ruth West, *Thea's Tarot* pamphlet, West Somerville, MA: Medusa Graphics, 1984.

The Winnipeg Tarot Co., *Winnipeg Tarot Co.: "Fortuna & Fabulation for All"* booklet, Winnipeg, MB: Finger in the Dyke Productions, 2010.